SCIENTIFIC AMERICAN™ *Critical Anthologies on Environment and Climate*™

CRITICAL PERSPECTIVES ON
ENVIRONMENTAL PROTECTION

Edited by Krista West

The Rosen Publishing Group, Inc., New York

Published in 2007 by The Rosen Publishing Group, Inc.
29 East 21st Street, New York, NY 10010

The articles in this book first appeared in the pages of *Scientific American*, as
follows: "Capturing Greenhouse Gases" by Howard Herzog, Baldur Eliasson,
and Olav Kaarstad, February 2000; "Paving Out Pollution" by Linda Wang,
February 2002; "Defusing the Global Warming Time Bomb" by James Hansen,
March 2004; "Profile: Mario Molina" by Sasha Nemecek, November 1997;
"Sewage Treatment Plants" by W. Wayt Gibbs, November 1995; "Growing
More Food with Less Water" by Sandra Postel, February 2001; "Cleaning Up the
River Rhine" by Karl-Geert Malle, January 1996; "Car Parts from Chickens" by
Diane Martindale, April 2000; "It's Not Easy Being Green" by Steven Ashley,
April 2002; "Can Nuclear Waste Be Stored Safely at Yucca Mountain?" by Chris
G. Whipple, June 1996; "A Case of the Vapors" by Rebecca Renner, July 2002;
"Sustaining the Amazon" by Marguerite Holloway, July 1993; "Can Sustainable
Management Save Tropical Forests?" by Richard E. Rice, Raymond E. Gullison,
and John W. Reid, April 1997; "Replumbing the Everglades" by Mark Alpert,
August 1999; "Endangered Again" by Tim Beardsley, October 1995; and in
the pages of *Scientific American Presents: The Oceans*, Fall 1998, as follows:
"The Promise and Perils of Aquaculture" by the Editors; "Giant Questions
about Shrimp" by the Editors; "Notes from an Adviser to the Shrimp Industry"
by Claude E. Boyd; "Comments from an Environmental Advocate" by Jason
W. Clay; and "Struggles with Salmon" by Krista McKinsey.

First Edition

Library of Congress Cataloging-in-Publication Data

Critical perspectives on environmental protection/edited by Krista West.—1st ed.
    p. cm.—(Scientific American critical anthologies on environment and climate)
Includes bibliographical references and index.
ISBN 1-4042-0691-4 (library binding)
1. Environmental protection—Juvenile literature. I. West, Krista. II. Series.
TD170.15.C75 2006
363.7—dc22

                                                                    2005031483

Manufactured in the United States of America

On the cover: Scientists wearing protective suits sampled lake water in 1994.

CONTENTS

Introduction

In 1962, a book about the effects of insecticides and pesticides on songbird populations throughout the United States started the modern movement to protect the environment. The book, entitled *Silent Spring*, presented evidence that industrial chemical pollution was harming wildlife and humans, and that its effects were being largely ignored by lawmakers.

The book was written by Rachel Carson, who grew up in Pennsylvania and is said to have inherited a love of nature from her mother. Carson studied marine biology in college and later worked as a science writer for the U.S. Bureau of Fisheries—an unusual job for a woman at that time. It was with this federal agency that she first learned of the harmful effects of some chemicals in nature.

By the time she wrote *Silent Spring*, Carson was already a well-known nature writer. But in that book, she convincingly argued that humans were controlling and destroying the natural world with careless technology, and she strongly criticized industries and government for ignoring the resulting chemical pollution problems. Little did Carson know that *Silent Spring* would set off a wave of environmental legislation to regulate such pollution.

In 1963, Carson herself testified before Congress and asked for new policies to protect human health and the environment. Shortly after that, Congress asked President John F. Kennedy to study the problem. The resulting report did many things. It supported Carson's suggestion that pesticides were poisoning the planet, it criticized government plans to get rid of some pests using chemical means, it called for a reduction in the use of certain pesticides suspected to be harmful, and it acknowledged the general lack of concern for human safety.

In a sense, Carson won the battle that began with *Silent Spring*. Today, almost half a century later, work to protect the environment continues—though it is often the center of political, scientific, and social debate. But regardless of one's opinion of the value of the environment, there's one fact that cannot be debated: there's no other planet quite like Earth.

Of all the planets in our solar system, Earth is the only one capable of supporting life as we know it. Many planets are too cold—Jupiter is −238 degrees Fahrenheit (−150 degrees Celsius); others are too hot—Venus is 847°F (453°C), hot enough to melt lead. Some planets have an unbreathable and sometimes toxic atmosphere, and the surfaces of some planets are often bombarded with harmful cosmic rays that could burn holes in your skin on contact. Perhaps the biggest and most important factor is that there is no water on other planets that we have found—and without water, life as we know it is impossible.

From this knowledge, it seems clear that a good planet is hard to find. And as human populations grow—there are about 6.5 billion humans on the planet and counting—we are demanding more and more from our unique planet. Humans have long used Earth's natural resources to survive. A natural resource is something that occurs naturally in the world and has economic value, such as timber, fish, minerals, and freshwater. This book is divided into four chapters based on Earth's four main categories of natural resources: air, water, land, and life.

Over time, Earth's air has become polluted, mainly with chemicals produced by cars and the burning of fossil fuels. But one type of pollution is a big concern: heat. We may not think of heat as a type of pollution, but warmer temperatures have the power to change our planet drastically over time. Understanding the causes, effects, and control of heat pollution, known generally as global warming, is one of the largest concerns in environmental protection of the air.

Earth's water resources face the threat of pollution in two ways: water as a garbage dump and water used in agriculture. Natural bodies of water such as rivers and seas are sometimes used as dumping grounds for things like sewage and industrial chemicals. In a different way, freshwater is a resource used to grow food and is sometimes polluted by waste from land and fish farms. On both fronts, environmental protection of Earth's water is a fundamental concern.

The land on Earth faces one of the most visible types of pollution: the garbage dump. Garbage from human activities—including everything from everyday trash to nuclear waste—often ends up buried on Earth's surface. Some of this garbage can be reduced and recycled, but the rest has to be stored somewhere for the long run. How to deal with waste disposal responsibly is a major issue in environmental protection of the land.

Life on Earth faces both direct and indirect threats. Life that is used as a natural resource (such as fish and forests) is directly affected by human actions. Life that is losing its home to human development (habitat loss) or harmed by human pollution (such as pesticides) is indirectly impacted by humans. In either case, some environmental protection practices are in place to preserve these resources. And more are being created every day.

To understand exactly which parts of Earth need protection and how to protect them, we turn to science. First, we need to know what something looked like in the past—what is "normal" for different parts of Earth. Second, we need to know the current state of things—the overall health of fish populations, for example. And last, we need to figure out ways to cure or treat any problems we find—often the hardest and most controversial part. At each step in determining what needs protection and how to protect it, science is a key tool for gathering knowledge.

When *Silent Spring* was first published nearly fifty years ago, the scientific evidence showing the harmful effects of pesticides on birds was already in the works. One pesticide called dichloro-diphenyl-trichloroethane (DDT) was widely used after World War II (1939–1945) to kill mosquitoes that potentially carried diseases such as malaria and typhus. Carson pointed out that DDT could cause cancer and harm bird reproduction by thinning egg shells, ultimately killing baby birds and preventing the population from reproducing.

After the science of DDT's harmful effects was better understood, the chemical was banned from use in the United States. Today, DDT is still used in countries where the threat of mosquitoes carrying diseases is greater than the environmental toxicity potential. But science has yet to find the ultimate cure: replacing DDT with a pesticide that takes care of the mosquitoes without harming the rest of the environment.

Without science, it is not likely we could effectively protect the environment. We have to know what was here and what is here now before we can protect anything. As Carson wrote, "The more clearly we can focus our attention on the wonders and realities of the universe about us, the less taste we shall have for destruction." We need science to focus our attention. This book is a collection of scientific articles to get you started in that direction. —*KW*

1 Air

The air that makes up Earth's atmosphere contains more carbon dioxide than it should. Carbon dioxide is the gas we exhale when we breathe. It is also the colorless and odorless gas that is given off when hydrocarbons such as coal, oil, and natural gas are burned for energy.

A certain amount of carbon dioxide and other gases in the atmosphere is natural. When these gases are balanced correctly, they help trap the sun's heat near the surface of the planet and maintain a temperature that is comfortable for life. When these gases (collectively called greenhouse gases, which include carbon dioxide, methane, water vapor, nitrous oxide, chlorofluoro-carbons, and ozone) are out of balance, the temperature of Earth begins to rise.

The level of carbon dioxide is currently out of balance as a result of human activity (for example, burning coal, oil, and natural gas). Over the past 150 years, human burning of fossil fuels has increased the amount of carbon dioxide in the atmosphere by almost one-third, or 30 percent.

The authors of the following article suggest trapping this extra carbon dioxide before it has a chance to get into the atmosphere, then storing it underground and in the oceans to prevent the warming of the atmosphere. Since 1996, Statoil, a company off the coast of Norway, has been giving this project a try. So far, the project seems to be working. There haven't been any unusual gas leaks and Statoil has won some awards for treating the environment well. —KW

"Capturing Greenhouse Gases"
by Howard Herzog, Baldur Eliasson, and Olav Kaarstad
Scientific American, February 2000

The debate over climate change has shifted. Until very recently, scientists still deliberated whether human activity was altering the global climate. Specifically, was the release of greenhouse gases, which trap heat radiating from the earth's surface, to blame? With scientific evidence mounting in favor of the affirmative, the discussion is now turning to what steps society can take to protect our climate.

One solution almost certainly will not succeed: running out of fossil fuels—namely, coal, oil and natural gas. Morris Adelman, professor emeritus at the Massachusetts Institute of Technology and expert on the economics of oil and gas, has consistently made this point for 30 years. In the past century and a half, since the beginning of the industrial age, the concentration of carbon dioxide in the atmosphere has risen by almost one third, from 280 to 370 parts per million (ppm)— primarily as a result of burning fossil fuels. In the 1990s, on average, humans discharged 1.5 ppm of carbon dioxide annually; with each passing year, the rate increased. Even though humans release other greenhouse gases, such as methane and nitrous oxide, experts project that carbon dioxide emissions will account for about two thirds of potential global warming. As apprehension has grown regarding the possible hazards of a changing global climate, environmental groups, governments and certain industries have been trying to reduce the level of greenhouse gases in the atmosphere, often by promoting energy efficiency and alternative energy sources—for instance, wind or solar power.

Realistically, however, fossil fuels are cheap and plentiful and will be powering our cars, homes and factories well into the 21st century and possibly beyond. Worries about diminishing fuel supplies have surfaced periodically over the past 100 years, but continuing improvements in both oil exploration and production technology should keep the fuel flowing for decades to come. Furthermore, since the adoption of the first international treaty designed to stabilize greenhouse gas emissions, signed at the 1992 Earth Summit in Rio de Janeiro, the global demand for fossil fuels has actually increased. Today more than 85 percent of the world's commercial energy needs are supplied by fossil fuels. Although policies that promote energy efficiency and alternative energy sources are crucial to mitigating climate change, they are only one part of the solution.

Indeed, even if society were to cut back the use of fossil fuels today, the planet would still most likely experience significant repercussions as a result of past emissions. The climate's response time is slow, and carbon dioxide remains in the atmosphere for a century or more if left to nature's devices. Therefore, we must have a portfolio of technology options to adequately reduce the accelerating buildup of greenhouse gases. Significant research and development efforts are already exploring ways to improve energy efficiency and increase the use of fuels with no carbon content (renewable energy sources or nuclear power). But a third approach is attracting notice as people recognize that the first two options will simply not be sufficient: carbon sequestration, the idea of finding reservoirs where carbon dioxide can be stored rather than allowing it to build up in the atmosphere.

Our strategy may surprise some readers. Sequestering carbon is often connected to planting trees: trees (and vegetation in general) absorb carbon dioxide from the air as they grow and hold on to that carbon for their lifetime [*see box on page 15*]. Scientists estimate that, all together, plants currently retain about 600 gigatons of carbon, with another 1,600 gigatons in the soil.

Plants and soils could perhaps sequester another 100 gigatons or more of carbon, but additional sinks will be needed to meet the challenge of escalating greenhouse gas emissions. So during the past 10 years,

Plant a Tree
Another Option for Storing Carbon
Needs Only Sun and Water

For over a decade, an organized carbon sequestration project has been under way in the deforested regions and farmlands of Guatemala. No underground pipes or pumping stations are required—just trees. As the plants grow, they absorb carbon dioxide from the atmosphere, which they store as carbon in the form of wood. Hoping to capitalize on this natural vehicle for sequestering carbon, companies and governments have initiated reforestation, afforestation (planting trees on land not previously forested) and agroforestry (integrating trees with agricultural crops) efforts as a way to meet obligations set forth in the Kyoto Protocol, the international environmental treaty on lowering greenhouse gas emissions.

In 1988 AES, a U.S.-based electrical company, pioneered the first forestry project designed to offset carbon dioxide emissions. At the time, AES was about to build a new coal-fired power plant in Connecticut, which was expected to release 52 million tons of carbon dioxide during its 40-year life span. Working in Guatemala with the World Resources Institute (WRI) and the relief organization CARE, AES created community woodlots, introduced agroforestry practices and trained forest-fire brigades. According to WRI calculations, up to 58 million tons of

continued on following page

continued from previous page

carbon dioxide will be absorbed over the lifetime of the project. Currently more than a dozen such programs are under way on some four million hectares of forest land, including areas in the U.S., Norway, Brazil, Malaysia, Russia and Australia.

According to recent estimates, forests around the globe today store nearly one trillion tons of carbon. Scientists calculate that to balance current carbon dioxide emissions, people would have to plant new forests every year covering an area of land equivalent to the whole of India. Forestry projects are not a quick-fix solution, but they do offer many benefits, ranging from better habitats for wildlife to increased employment. Nevertheless, the potential for trees to serve as a reservoir for carbon is limited, and the approach has its drawbacks. Tree plantations drain native plant biodiversity and can disturb local communities, forcing them to relocate. As with many proposed solutions to climate change, trees will be effective only as one part of a global commitment to reduce greenhouse gas emissions.   —*Diane Martindale*

the three of us have explored another possibility: capturing carbon dioxide from stationary sources— for example, a chemical factory or an electric power plant—and injecting it into the ocean or underground. We are not alone in our efforts but are part of a worldwide research community that includes the

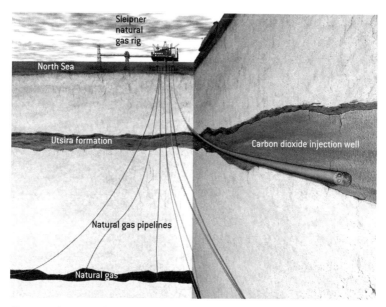

Deep underground, some 1,000 meters below the bottom of the North Sea, carbon dioxide is pumped into the sandstone reservoir known as the Utsira Formation, where it can be stored for thousands of years. To avoid Norway's carbon dioxide tax, the owners of the Sleipner natural gas rig, located some 240 kilometers from the Norwegian coast, now bury the greenhouse gas that would otherwise be released from the rig into the atmosphere.

International Energy Agency (IEA) Greenhouse Gas Research and Development Program, as well as government and industry programs.

A New Approach in Norway

Sleipner offshore oil and natural gas field is in the middle of the North Sea, some 240 kilometers off the coast of Norway. Workers on one of the natural gas rigs there inject 20,000 tons of carbon dioxide each

text continues on page 20

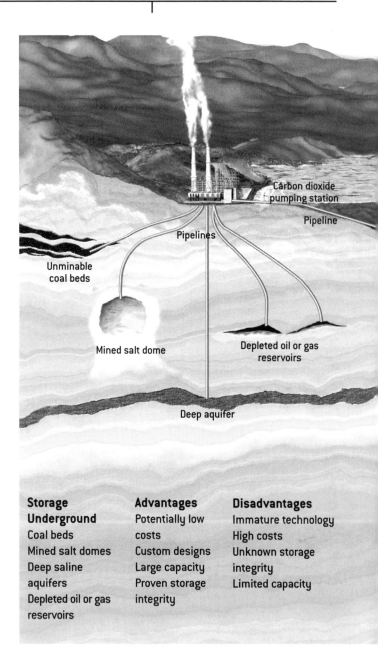

Storage Underground	Advantages	Disadvantages
Coal beds	Potentially low costs	Immature technology
Mined salt domes	Custom designs	High costs
Deep saline aquifers	Large capacity	Unknown storage integrity
Depleted oil or gas reservoirs	Proven storage integrity	Limited capacity

Storage sites for carbon dioxide in the ground and deep sea should help keep the greenhouse gas out of the atmosphere where it now

STORING CARBON DIOXIDE UNDERGROUND AND IN THE OCEAN

Carbon dioxide
pumping station

Towed pipe

1,000 m

Dry ice

Droplet plume

2,000 m

3,000 m

Carbon dioxide lake

Storage in Ocean	Advantages	Disadvantages
Droplet plume	Minimal environmental	Some leakage
Towed pipe	effects	Some leakage
Dry ice	Minimal environmental	High costs
Carbon dioxide lake	effects	Immature
	Simple technology	technology
	Carbon will remain in	
	ocean for thousands	
	of years	

contributes to climate change. The various options must be scrutinized for cost, safety and potential environmental effects.

continued from page 17

week into the pores of a sandstone layer 1,000 meters below the seabed. When the injection at Sleipner began in October 1996, it marked the first instance of carbon dioxide being stored in a geologic formation because of climate considerations.

How did this venture come about? One reservoir at Sleipner contains natural gas diluted with 9 percent carbon dioxide—too much for it to be attractive to customers, who generally accept no more than 2.5 percent. So, as is common practice at other natural gas fields around the world, an on-site chemical plant extracted the excess carbon dioxide. At any other installation, this carbon dioxide would simply be released to the atmosphere. But the owners of the Sleipner field—Statoil (where one of us, Kaarstad, works as a researcher), Exxon, Norsk Hydro and Elf—decided to sequester the greenhouse gas by first compressing it and then pumping it down a well into a 200-meter-thick sandstone layer, known as the Utsira Formation, which was originally filled with saltwater. The nearly one million tons of carbon dioxide sequestered at Sleipner last year may not seem large, but in the small country of Norway, it amounts to about 3 percent of total emissions to the atmosphere of this greenhouse gas.

The principal motivation for returning carbon to the ground at Sleipner was the Norwegian offshore carbon dioxide tax, which in 1996 amounted to $50 for every ton of the gas emitted (as of January 1, 2000, the tax was lowered to $38 per ton). The investment in the compression equipment and carbon dioxide well totaled around $80 million. In comparison, if the carbon dioxide had been emitted to the atmosphere, the companies would have owed about $50 million each year between 1996 and 1999. Thus, the savings paid off the investment in only a year and a half.

In other parts of the world, companies are planning similar projects. In the South China Sea, the Natuna field contains natural gas with nearly 71 percent carbon dioxide. Once this field has been developed commercially, the excess carbon dioxide will be sequestered. Other studies are investigating the possibility of storing captured carbon dioxide underground, including within liquefied natural gas installations at the Gorgon field on Australia's Northwest Shelf and the Snøhvit ("Snow White") gas field in the Barents Sea off northern Norway, as well as the oil fields of Alaska's North Slope.

In all the projects now under way or in development, carbon dioxide must be captured for commercial reasons—for instance, to purify natural gas before it can be sold. The choice facing the companies involved is therefore between releasing the greenhouse gas to the atmosphere or storing it. They are not deciding whether to collect the carbon dioxide in the first place. We expect that more such companies needing to reduce carbon dioxide emissions will opt for sequestration in the future, but convincing other businesses to capture carbon dioxide emissions from large point sources such as electric power plants is more difficult because of the costs associated with carbon dioxide collection.

text continues on page 24

The Basics: Burying Carbon Dioxide
The Authors Review Carbon Sequestration Technology

What is carbon sequestration? The idea is to store the greenhouse gas carbon dioxide in natural reservoirs rather than allowing it to build up in the atmosphere. Although sequestering carbon is often connected to planting trees, we are investigating the possibility of capturing carbon dioxide from stationary sources—an electric power plant, for example—and injecting it into the ocean or underground.

Where exactly will the carbon dioxide be stored? It can be pumped into underground geologic formations, such as unminable coal beds, depleted oil or gas wells, or saline aquifers, in a process that is essentially the reverse of pumping oil up from below the earth's surface. Engineers are also looking into the possibility of bubbling carbon dioxide directly into the ocean at concentrations that will not affect the surrounding ecosystem and at depths that will ensure it remains in the ocean.

How will scientists make certain it is stored safely? Making sure carbon dioxide will be stored in a safe and environmentally sound manner is one of our primary goals. Memories of the 1986 Lake Nyos tragedy in

Cameroon (in which a huge bubble of carbon dioxide erupted from the lake, suffocating some 1,700 people), raise the issue of safety, particularly for underwater storage. Yet the situation in the lake was entirely different than the scenario we envision for carbon sequestration in the ocean. A small lake simply cannot hold a large amount of carbon dioxide, so the Nyos eruption was inevitable. There are no such limitations in the oceans. In the case of underground storage, nature has demonstrated a safe track record: reservoirs such as the McElmo Dome in southwestern Colorado have held large quantities of carbon dioxide for centuries.

Are there any active carbon sequestration projects today? The Sleipner natural gas rig off the coast of Norway currently pumps carbon dioxide into a saline aquifer 1,000 meters below the seafloor. Although Sleipner is the only sequestration project driven solely by climatic change considerations, other commercial projects demonstrate the technology. More than a dozen power plants capture carbon dioxide from their flue gas, including the Shady Point, Okla., plant built by the international engineering company ABB. And at over 65 oil wells in the U.S., companies inject the gas underground to enhance the efficiency of oil drilling.

continued from page 21

Underground or Underwater

The technology for pumping carbon dioxide into the ground is actually well established—it is essentially the reverse of pumping oil and natural gas out of the ground. In fact, the practice is common at many oil fields today. Injecting carbon dioxide into an existing oil reservoir increases the mobility of the oil inside and thereby enhances the well's productivity. During 1998, U.S. oil field workers pumped a total of about 43 million tons of carbon dioxide into the ground at more than 65 enhanced oil recovery (EOR) projects. Yet this quantity adds up to comparatively little carbon sequestration. In contrast, geologic formations, including saline aquifer formations (such as that at Sleipner), unminable coal beds, depleted oil or gas reservoirs, rock caverns and mined salt domes all around the world, can collectively hold hundreds if not thousands of gigatons of carbon.

Although geologic formations show great promise as storage sites, the largest potential reservoir for anthropogenic carbon dioxide is the deep ocean. Dissolved in its waters, the ocean holds an estimated 40,000 gigatons of carbon (compared with 750 gigatons in the atmosphere), but its capacity is much larger. Even if humans were to add to the ocean an amount of carbon dioxide equivalent to doubling the preindustrial atmospheric concentration of the gas, it would change the carbon content of the deep ocean by less than 2 percent. Indeed, slow-acting, natural processes will direct about 85 percent of present-day emissions into the oceans over hundreds of years. Our idea is to accelerate these events.

For ocean sequestration to be effective, the carbon dioxide must be injected into the sea below the thermocline—the layer of ocean between approximately 100 and 1,000 meters, in which water temperatures decrease dramatically with depth. The cooler, denser water below travels extremely slowly up through the thermocline. Therefore, the water beneath the thermocline may take centuries to mix with the surface waters, and any carbon dioxide below this boundary will be effectively trapped. In general, the deeper we inject the carbon dioxide, the longer it will take to reach the atmosphere.

Carbon dioxide can be introduced into seawater in two ways: dissolving it at moderate depths (from 1,000 to 2,000 meters) to form a dilute solution or injecting it below 3,000 meters to create what we call a carbon dioxide lake. The first strategy seeks to minimize local environmental effects by diluting the carbon dioxide, whereas the lake approach tries to maximize the length of time the carbon dioxide will reside in the ocean.

The concept of storing carbon dioxide in the ocean can be traced to a 1977 paper by Cesare Marchetti of the International Institute for Applied Systems Analysis in Laxenburg, Austria, who suggested that carbon dioxide could be piped into the waters of the Mediterranean Sea at Gibraltar, where it would naturally flow out into the Atlantic and be carried to the deep ocean. Even today building a pipe along the ocean floor to transport

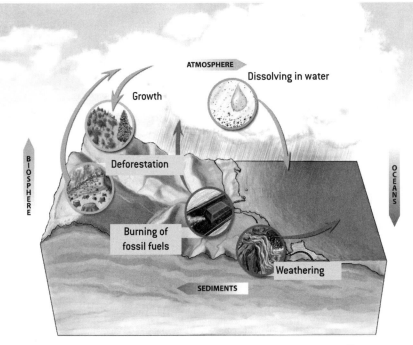

Natural stores of carbon exist in the atmosphere, oceans, sediments and biosphere; exchange between these reservoirs occurs in a variety of ways. When humans burn fossil fuels, we transfer carbon originally stored in the deep sediments into the atmosphere. The goal of carbon sequestration is to redirect carbon from the atmosphere into one of the other three reservoirs.

carbon dioxide to an appropriate depth remains one of the more realistic options for carbon sequestration. Other injection scenarios that have been suggested include dropping dry ice into the ocean from ships, introducing carbon dioxide at 1,000 meters through a pipe towed by a moving ship, and running a pipe down 3,000 meters or more to depressions in the seafloor.

Safe and Sound?

Despite the availability of the technology necessary to proceed with carbon storage in both terrestrial and oceanic reservoirs, we need to understand better what the consequences for the environment will be. Obviously, the process of storing carbon dioxide needs to be less damaging to the environment than the continued release of the greenhouse gas. In the case of underground storage, we must be sure to assess the long-term stability of any formation under consideration as a reservoir. The structural integrity of a site is important not only to ensure that the gas does not return to the atmosphere gradually but also because a sudden release of the carbon dioxide in a populated area could be catastrophic. Carbon dioxide is heavier than air, and a rapid, massive discharge of the gas would displace oxygen at the surface, suffocating people and wildlife. Fortunately, though, nature has stored carbon dioxide underground for millions of years in reservoirs such as McElmo Dome in southwestern Colorado, so we know there are ways to do it safely.

Ocean sequestration presents a different set of challenges. The leading concern is the repercussion it will have on the acidity of the ocean. Depending on the method of carbon dioxide release, the pH of seawater in the vicinity of an injection site could be between 5 and 7. (A pH of 7 is considered neutral; the pH of seawater is normally around 8.)

A large change in acidity could be harmful to organisms such as zooplankton, bacteria and bottom-dwelling creatures that cannot swim to less acidic waters. Research by one of us (Herzog) and M.I.T. colleague E. Eric Adams, however, suggests that keeping the concentration of carbon dioxide dilute could minimize or even eliminate problems with acidity. For example, a dilution factor of one part per million yields a change in pH of less than 0.1. This reduced concentration could easily be achieved by releasing the carbon dioxide as small droplets from a pipe on the seafloor or on a moving ship.

Over the next several years, the scientific community will be conducting a number of experiments to assess how large amounts of carbon dioxide can be stored in a safe and environmentally sound manner. In the summer of 2001, for instance, a team of researchers from the U.S., Japan, Switzerland, Norway, Canada and Australia will begin a study off the Kona Coast of Hawaii to examine the technical feasibility and environmental effects of carbon storage in the ocean. (Two of us are participating in this project, Herzog as a member of the technical committee and Eliasson as a member of the steering committee.)

Our plan is to run a series of about 10 tests over a period of two weeks, involving the release of carbon dioxide at a depth of 800 meters. We will be monitoring the resulting plume and taking measurements, including the pH of the water and the amount of dissolved inorganic carbon. These data will allow us to refine

text continues on page 35

A Breakthrough in Climate Change Policy?
by David W. Keith and Edward A. Parson

As a result of human activities, the atmospheric concentration of carbon dioxide has increased by 31 percent over the past two centuries. According to business-as-usual projections, it will reach twice the preindustrial level before 2100. Although there is little doubt that this increase will noticeably transform the climate, substantial uncertainties remain about the magnitude, timing and regional patterns of climate change; even less is known about the ecological, economic and social consequences.

Despite these uncertainties, an international consensus has emerged regarding the importance of preventing runaway levels of carbon dioxide in the atmosphere. An effort to stabilize the concentration of carbon dioxide at even double its preindustrial level—generally considered the lowest plausible target—will require reducing global carbon dioxide emissions by about 50 percent from projected levels by 2050. Not surprisingly, such an extreme reduction will require a fundamental reorganization of global energy systems.

Most current assessments of greenhouse gas emissions assume that the reductions will be achieved through a mix of increasing energy efficiency and switching to no fossil-fuel alternative energy sources, such as solar, wind, biomass or nuclear. In the accompanying article, "Capturing Greenhouse Gases," the authors review

continued on following page

continued from previous page

a radically different approach: burning fossil fuels without releasing carbon dioxide to the atmosphere by separating the carbon emissions and burying them underground or in the deep ocean. We believe this approach—termed carbon management—has fundamental implications for the economics and politics of climate change.

Stabilizing the carbon dioxide concentration at 550 parts per million (ppm)—double the preindustrial level—is widely considered an ambitious target for emissions control. Yet this concentration will still cause substantial climate change. The resulting environmental problems, however, will most likely have only a small effect on the world's overall economic output; rich countries in particular should emerge relatively unscathed. But the results for specific regions will be more pronounced, with some places benefiting and others suffering. For instance, although parts of the northern U.S. may enjoy warmer winters, entire ecosystems, such as the southwestern mountain forests, alpine meadows and certain coastal forests, may disappear from the continental U.S. These likely consequences—and more important, the possibility of unanticipated changes—are compelling reasons to try to stabilize concentrations below 550 ppm, if it can be done at an acceptable cost.

At present, the cost of holding concentrations to even 550 ppm through conventional means appears high, both in dollars and in other environmental problems. All nonfossil-fuel energy sources available today are expensive, and renewable sources have low power densities: they produce relatively little power for the amount of land required. Large-scale use of renewable energy could thereby harm our most precious environmental resource: land. Although technological advances should reduce the cost of renewables, little can be done to improve their power densities, which are intrinsic to the sources.

So must we conclude that reducing carbon emissions without causing other unacceptable environmental impacts will deliver a massive economic blow? Not necessarily. The crux of the cost problem is predicting how fast money-saving technical advances might develop in response to a carbon tax or some other form of regulation. Notably, most economic models used today to assess the cost of reducing emissions assume that innovation proceeds at its own pace and cannot be accelerated by policy. Under this assumption, delaying efforts to cut emissions makes sense because it will allow time to develop better technology that will lower the cost of reductions. Under the contrary assumption—which we regard as closer to the truth—innovation responds strongly to price and policy signals. In this case, early policy action on climate change is advantageous, because it would stimulate the innovations that reduce the cost of making large emission reductions.

continued on following page

continued from previous page

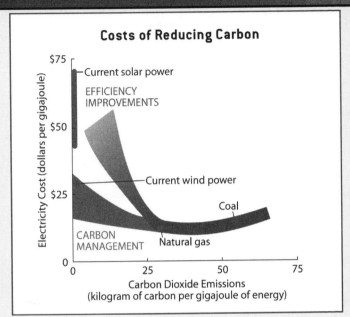

Costs of Reducing Carbon

Reducing carbon dioxide emissions by switching from coal to natural gas can save money. The authors argue that further reductions will be cheaper to make by carbon management than by solar power or by extreme efficiency improvements. Although wind power is relatively cheap, the land area required may preclude its widespread use.

Carbon management may be just such an innovation. Certain carbon management technologies are already available and appear to be significantly cheaper than renewables for generating electricity. To achieve deep reductions in greenhouse gas emissions, however, society must also start using carbon-free fuels, such as hydrogen, for transportation. Here the relative advantage of carbon management over renewables is even greater than in producing electricity. Furthermore, these technologies offer one significant advantage over alternative energy sources: because they are more compatible with the existing energy infrastructure, we expect their costs to fall more quickly than those of renewables.

Carbon management weakens the link between burning fossil fuels and releasing greenhouse gases, making the world's economic dependence on fossil fuels more sustainable. This gives carbon management a crucial advantage: by reducing the threat to fossil-fuel industries and fossil-fuel-rich nations, carbon management may ease current political deadlocks. Stated bluntly, if society adopts carbon management widely, existing fossil-fuel-dependent industries and nations may continue to operate profitably both in present energy markets and in new markets that develop around carbon management, making them more willing to tolerate policies that pursue substantial reduction of atmospheric emissions.

Environmentalists, however, are likely to find carbon management profoundly divisive for several reasons. Carbon sequestration is only as good as the reservoirs in which the carbon is stored. The unfortunate history of toxic and nuclear waste disposal has left many reasonable people skeptical of expert claims about the longevity of

continued on following page

continued from previous page

underground carbon disposal. As researchers assess the safety of proposed carbon reservoirs both underground and in the ocean, they must address such skepticism evenhandedly.

Perhaps even more disconcerting for environmentalists, though, is that carbon management collides with a deeply rooted belief that continued dependence on fossil fuels is an intrinsic problem, for which the only acceptable solution is renewable energy. Carbon management was first proposed as "geoengineering," a label it now shares with proposals to engineer the global climate, for example, by injecting aerosols into the stratosphere to reflect solar radiation and cool the earth's surface. Many environmentalists hold a reasonable distaste for large-scale technical fixes, arguing that it would be better to use energy sources that do not require such massive clean-up efforts.

Carbon management is a promising technology, but it remains unproved. And caution is certainly wise: the history of energy technologies is littered with options once touted as saviors that now play at most minor roles (for example, nuclear energy). Exploring the potential of either carbon management or renewable energy will require political and economic action now—that is, greater support for basic energy research and carbon taxes or equivalent policy measures that give firms incentives to develop and commercialize innovations that reduce emissions at a reasonable cost. It may be that carbon management will allow the world—at long last—to make deep cuts in carbon dioxide emissions at a politically acceptable cost. Indeed, for the next several decades, carbon management may be our best shot at protecting the global climate.

DAVID W. KEITH and EDWARD A. PARSON often collaborate on environmental policy research. Keith is an assistant professor in the department of engineering and public policy at Carnegie Mellon University. Parson is an associate professor at the John F. Kennedy School of Government at Harvard University.

continued from page 28

computer models and thereby generalize the results of this experiment to predict environmental responses more accurately. We are also interested in what technical design works best to rapidly dilute the small droplets of carbon dioxide.

Money Matters

Along with questions of environmental safety and practicality, we must look at how much carbon sequestration will cost. Because electricity-generating power plants account for about one third of all carbon dioxide released to the atmosphere worldwide and because such plants are large, concentrated sources of emissions, they provide a logical target for implementing carbon sequestration. Furthermore, such plants have had experience reducing pollutants in the past. (Notably, though, attention has primarily focused on controlling such contaminants as particulate matter, sulfur oxides, nitrogen oxides or even carbon monoxide—but not on carbon dioxide itself.)

Devices known as electrostatic precipitators, first introduced in the 1910s, helped to clean up the particles emitted from burning fossil fuels while raising the price of electricity only modestly. Today a modern power plant that includes state-of-the-art environmental cleanup equipment for particulates, sulfur oxides and nitrogen oxides costs up to 30 percent more to install than a plant without such equipment. This environmental equipment adds only between 0.1 and 0.5 of a cent per kilowatt-hour to the price of the electricity generated.

Because the exhaust gases of fossil-fueled power plants contain low concentrations of carbon dioxide (typically ranging from 3 to 15 percent), it would not be economical to funnel the entire exhaust stream into storage sites. The first step, therefore, should be to concentrate the carbon dioxide found in emissions. Unfortunately, with existing equipment this step turns out to be the most expensive. Thus, developing technology that lowers these costs is a major goal.

The most common method for separating carbon dioxide involves mixing a solution of dilute monoethanolamine (MEA) with the flue gases inside the absorption tower of a plant designed to capture the greenhouse gas. The carbon dioxide in the exhaust reacts with the MEA solution at room temperature to form a new, loosely bound compound. This compound is then heated in a second column, the stripping tower, to approximately 120 degrees C to release the carbon dioxide. The gaseous carbon dioxide product is then compressed, dried, chilled, liquefied and purified (if necessary); the liquid MEA solution is recycled. Currently this technology works well, but it must become more energy efficient if it is to be applied to large-scale carbon sequestration. Today only a handful of power plants, including one built in Shady Point, Okla., by ABB (where Eliasson serves as head of global change research), capture carbon dioxide from their flue gases. The carbon dioxide is then sold for commercial applications, such as freeze-drying chicken or carbonating beer and soda.

Another application for captured carbon dioxide offers a number of possible benefits. Methanol can be used as fuel even now. Generating this cleaner source of energy from captured carbon dioxide and hydrogen extracted from carbon-free sources would be more expensive than producing methanol from natural gas, as is currently done. But by reusing carbon dioxide—and by giving it a market value—this procedure ought to reduce overall emissions, provide an incentive to lower the costs of carbon dioxide–capture technology and help start a transition to more routine use of cleaner fuels.

Scientists, policymakers and the public must deal with the continuing importance of coal, oil and natural gas as a source of energy, even in a world constrained by concerns about climate change. The basic technology needed to use these fuels in a climate-friendly manner does exist. Current equipment for capturing carbon dioxide from power plants would raise the cost of generating electricity by 50 to 100 percent. But because sequestration does not affect the cost of electricity transmission and distribution (a significant portion of consumers' electricity bills), delivered prices will rise less, by about 30 to 50 percent. Research into better separation technologies should lead to lowered costs.

What needs to happen for carbon sequestration to become common practice? First, researchers need to verify the feasibility of the various proposed storage sites, in an open and publicly acceptable process. Second, we need leadership from industry and government to demonstrate these technologies on a large enough scale. Finally, we need improved technology to reduce costs associated with carbon dioxide separation from power plants. The Sleipner project has shown that carbon sequestration represents a realistic option to reduce carbon dioxide emissions when an economic incentive exists. During the past 100 years, our energy supply system has undergone revolutionary changes—from a stationary economy based on coal and steam to a mobile economy based on liquid fuels, gas and electricity. The changes over the next 100 years promise to be no less revolutionary.

The Authors

Howard Herzog, Baldur Eliasson and Olav Kaarstad met in Amsterdam in March 1992 at the First International Conference on Carbon Dioxide Removal. Herzog, a principal research engineer at the Massachusetts Institute of Technology Energy Laboratory, is the primary author of a 1997 U.S. Department of Energy White Paper on carbon sequestration. Eliasson, head of ABB's Energy and Global Change Program, is the Swiss representative to as well as vice chairman of the International Energy Agency's Greenhouse Gas Research and Development Program. Kaarstad, principal research adviser in the area of energy and environment at the Norwegian oil and gas company Statoil, is currently involved in the ongoing carbon dioxide–injection project at the Sleipner field in the North Sea.

The air in large cities is often polluted with nitrogen oxides—a group of gases commonly found in smog and acid rain that can cause breathing problems in humans. But once released into the air, nitrogen oxides are very hard to catch. A new trick may use the sun's energy to break down these often colorless, odorless gases and render them harmless.

The new trick is titanium dioxide, a compound that begins a series of tiny chemical reactions to

*suck nitrogen oxides out of the air. Here's how it
works: First, titanium dioxide uses sunlight to
break down water molecules (found naturally in
the air) into little magnetlike particles. Next,
these little magnet particles, called ions, turn
harmful nitrogen oxides into harmless particles.
Last, the new, harmless particles are washed
away by the rain.*

*If it works, titanium dioxide could be a sort of
sunscreen for cities—we could slather it on urban
streets and sidewalks to protect ourselves from
air pollution. Hong Kong is already giving it a try,
and titanium dioxide is credited with removing
90 percent of the harmful nitrogen oxides from
the city's air. —KW*

"Paving Out Pollution"
by Linda Wang
Scientific American, **February 2002**

Buildings, roads and sidewalks have developed an
appetite for air pollution. Researchers in Japan and
Hong Kong are testing construction materials coated
with titanium dioxide—the stuff of white paint and
toothpaste—to see how well they can fight pollution.

Better known as a pigment for whiteness, titanium
dioxide can clear the air because it is an efficient
photocatalyst: it speeds the breakdown of water vapor
by ultraviolet light. The results of this reaction are
hydroxyl radicals, which attack both inorganic and

organic compounds, and turn them into molecules that can be harmlessly washed away with the next rainfall. But it wouldn't work to smear toothpaste on the sidewalk—the titanium dioxide crystals in such applications are too large (about 20 to 250 nanometers wide). The width of the pollution-fighting form is about seven nanometers, offering much more surface area for photocatalysis.

In the early 1970s researchers from the University of Tokyo described titanium dioxide's photocatalytic abilities. Since then, scientists have exploited the compound to kill bacteria on hospital surfaces and to treat contaminated water. Fighting nitrogen oxide on the streets is the latest twist. In Hong Kong, concrete slabs coated with titanium dioxide removed up to 90 percent of nitrogen oxides, most commonly spewed from older cars and diesel trucks and a contributor to smog, acid rain and other environmental headaches. In taking care of the contaminants, a coating of titanium dioxide did in minutes what the environment does in months, says Jimmy Chai-Mei Yu, a chemist at the Chinese University of Hong Kong. Moreover, he adds, because titanium dioxide is a catalyst, it could last forever.

Despite its promise, the compound is no magical cure. "The big problem with titanium dioxide is that it doesn't absorb sunlight very well," says Carl Koval, a chemist at the University of Colorado at Boulder. Only 3 percent of sunlight falls into the range needed for the titanium dioxide to work, points out Adam Heller, a chemical engineer at the University of Texas at Austin.

A recent advance by Ryoji Asahi of Toyota Central R&D Laboratories in Nagakute, Japan, boosted the efficiency to 10 percent, but, Heller notes, "it's still a small fraction of the sunlight."

And although titanium dioxide is relatively inexpensive, paving roads and coating buildings with this substance could add up. "The countries with the most air pollution will benefit the most from this technology," Yu observes, "but unfortunately those are the countries that won't be able to afford it."

Linda Wang is a writer based in Chicago.

The air surrounding Earth has warmed in recent decades. Scientists are confident that this warming is caused by human-made air pollution, which includes carbon dioxide and other gases. The question is, what are we going to do about it?

The author of this article, James Hansen, says we better act fast because the devastating effects of global warming will occur sooner than we think. He is most concerned about melting sea ice, which could raise sea levels and wipe out coastal towns and populations. But he says there is still time to act.

Hansen is just one of hundreds of scientists warning the world of global warming—but he's

*an important one. Hansen was the first scientist
to bring the issue to the world's attention when
he testified before Congress in 1980. At the time,
not many people believed him, and a huge debate
ensued over whether or not global warming was
real. Today, no credible sources debate the reality
of global warming—it is real. But they do debate
how it happens and what we can do about it.
Here's one idea. —KW*

"Defusing the Global Warming Time Bomb"
by James Hansen
Scientific American, March 2004

A paradox in the notion of human-made global warming
became strikingly apparent to me one summer afternoon
in 1976 on Jones Beach, Long Island. Arriving at
midday, my wife, son and I found a spot near the water
to avoid the scorching hot sand. As the sun sank in the
late afternoon, a brisk wind from the ocean whipped
up whitecaps. My son and I had goose bumps as we
ran along the foamy shoreline and watched the
churning waves.

That same summer Andy Lacis and I, along with
other colleagues at the NASA Goddard Institute for
Space Studies, had estimated the effects of greenhouse
gases on climate. It was well known by then that human-
made greenhouse gases, especially carbon dioxide and
chlorofluorocarbons (CFCs), were accumulating in the
atmosphere. These gases are a climate "forcing," a

perturbation imposed on the energy budget of the planet. Like a blanket, they absorb infrared (heat) radiation that would otherwise escape from the earth's surface and atmosphere to space.

Our group had calculated that these human-made gases were heating the earth's surface at a rate of almost two watts per square meter. A miniature Christmas tree bulb dissipates about one watt, mostly in the form of heat. So it was as if humans had placed two of these tiny bulbs over every square meter of the earth's surface, burning night and day.

The paradox that this result presented was the contrast between the awesome forces of nature and the tiny lightbulbs. Surely their feeble heating could not command the wind and waves or smooth our goose bumps. Even their imperceptible heating of the ocean surface must be quickly dissipated to great depths, so it must take many years, perhaps centuries, for the ultimate surface warming to be achieved.

This seeming paradox has now been largely resolved through study of the history of the earth's climate, which reveals that small forces, maintained long enough, can cause large climate change. And, consistent with the historical evidence, the earth has begun to warm in recent decades at a rate predicted by climate models that take account of the atmospheric accumulation of human-made greenhouse gases. The warming is having noticeable impacts as glaciers are retreating worldwide, Arctic sea ice has thinned, and spring comes about one week earlier than when I grew up in the 1950s.

Overview/*Global Warming*

- At present, our most accurate knowledge about climate sensitivity is based on data from the earth's history, and this evidence reveals that small forces, maintained long enough, can cause large climate change.
- Human-made forces, especially greenhouse gases, soot and other small particles, now exceed natural forces, and the world has begun to warm at a rate predicted by climate models.
- The stability of the great ice sheets on Greenland and Antarctica and the need to preserve global coastlines set a low limit on the global warming that will constitute "dangerous anthropogenic interference" with climate.
- Halting global warming requires urgent, unprecedented international cooperation, but the needed actions are feasible and have additional benefits for human health, agriculture and the environment.

Yet many issues remain unresolved. How much will climate change in coming decades? What will be the practical consequences? What, if anything, should we do about it? The debate over these questions is highly charged because of the inherent economic stakes.

Objective analysis of global warming requires quantitative knowledge of three issues: the sensitivity of the climate system to forcings, the forcings that humans are introducing, and the time required for climate to respond. All these issues can be studied with global climate models, which are numerical simulations on computers. But our most accurate knowledge about climate sensitivity, at least so far, is based on empirical data from the earth's history.

The Lessons of History

Over the past few million years the earth's climate has swung repeatedly between ice ages and warm interglacial periods. A 400,000-year record of temperature is preserved in the Antarctic ice sheet, which, except for coastal fringes, escaped melting even in the warmest interglacial periods. This record [*see box on page 47*] suggests that the present interglacial period (the Holocene), now about 12,000 years old, is already long of tooth.

The natural millennial climate swings are associated with slow variations of the earth's orbit induced by the gravity of other planets, mainly Jupiter and Saturn (because they are so heavy) and Venus (because it comes so close). These perturbations hardly affect the annual mean solar energy striking the earth, but they alter the geographical and seasonal distribution of incoming solar energy, or insolation, as much as 20 percent. The insolation changes, over long periods, affect the building and melting of ice sheets.

Insolation and climate changes also affect uptake and release of carbon dioxide and methane by plants,

400,000 Years of Climate Change

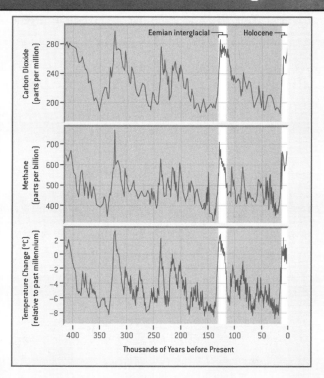

Antarctic ice has preserved a 400,000-year record of temperature and of levels of carbon dioxide and methane in the atmosphere. Scientists study gases trapped in air bubbles in the ice—generally using ice cores extracted from the ice sheet and transported to a laboratory. The historical record provides us with two critical measures: Comparison of the current interglacial period (the Holocene) with the most recent ice age (20,000 years ago) gives an accurate measure of climate sensitivity

continued on following page

continued from previous page

to forcings. The temperature in the previous interglacial period (the Eemian), when sea level was several meters higher than today, defines an estimate of the warming that today's civilization would consider to be dangerous anthropogenic interference with climate.

soil and the ocean. Climatologists are still developing a quantitative understanding of the mechanisms by which the ocean and land release carbon dioxide and methane as the earth warms, but the paleoclimate data are already a gold mine of information. The most critical insight that the ice age climate swings provide is an empirical measure of climate sensitivity.

The composition of the ice age atmosphere is known precisely from air bubbles trapped as the Antarctic and Greenland ice sheets and numerous mountain glaciers built up from annual snowfall. Furthermore, the geographical distributions of the ice sheets, vegetation cover and coastlines during the ice age are well mapped. From these data we know that the change of climate forcing between the ice age and today was about 6.5 watts per square meter. This forcing maintains a global temperature change of 5 degrees Celsius (9 degrees Fahrenheit), implying a climate sensitivity of 0.75 ± 0.25 degrees C per watt per square meter. Climate models yield a similar climate sensitivity. The empirical result is more precise and reliable, however, because it includes all the processes operating in the real world, even those we have not yet been smart enough to include in the models.

The paleodata provide another important insight. Changes of the earth's orbit instigate climate change, but they operate by altering atmosphere and surface properties and thus the planetary energy balance. These atmosphere and surface properties are now influenced more by humans than by our planet's orbital variations.

Climate-Forcing Agents Today

The largest change of climate forcings in recent centuries is caused by human-made greenhouse gases. Greenhouse gases in the atmosphere absorb heat radiation rather than letting it escape into space. In effect, they make the proverbial blanket thicker, returning more heat toward the ground rather than letting it escape to space. The earth then is radiating less energy to space than it absorbs from the sun. This temporary planetary energy imbalance results in the earth's gradual warming.

Because of the large capacity of the oceans to absorb heat, it takes the earth about a century to approach a new balance—that is, for it to once again receive the same amount of energy from the sun that it radiates to space. And of course the balance is reset at a higher temperature. In the meantime, before it achieves this equilibrium, more forcings may be added.

The single most important human-made greenhouse gas is carbon dioxide, which comes mainly from burning fossil fuels (coal, oil and gas). Yet the combined effect of the other human-made gases is comparable. These other gases, especially tropospheric ozone and its precursors, including methane, are ingredients in smog that damage human health and agricultural productivity.

Aerosols (fine particles in the air) are the other main human-made climate forcing. Their effect is more complex. Some "white" aerosols, such as sulfates arising from sulfur in fossil fuels, are highly reflective and thus reduce solar heating of the earth; however, black carbon (soot), a product of incomplete combustion of fossil fuels, biofuels and outdoor biomass burning, absorbs sunlight and thus heats the atmosphere. This aerosol direct climate forcing is uncertain by at least 50 percent, in part because aerosol amounts are not well measured and in part because of their complexity.

Aerosols also cause an indirect climate forcing by altering the properties of clouds. The resulting brighter, longer-lived clouds reduce the amount of sunlight absorbed by the earth, so the indirect effect of aerosols is a negative forcing that causes cooling.

Other human-made climate forcings include replacement of forests by cropland. Forests are dark even with snow on the ground, so their removal reduces solar heating.

Natural forcings, such as volcanic eruptions and fluctuations of the sun's brightness, probably have little trend on a timescale of 1,000 years. But evidence of a small solar brightening over the past 150 years implies a climate forcing of a few tenths of a watt per square meter.

The net value of the forcings added since 1850 is 1.6 ± 1.0 watts per square meter. Despite the large uncertainties, there is evidence that this estimated net forcing is approximately correct. One piece of evidence is the close agreement of observed global temperature during the past several decades with climate models driven by these forcings. More fundamentally, the observed heat gain by the world ocean in the past 50 years is consistent with the estimated net climate forcing.

Global Warming

Global average surface temperature has increased about 0.75 degree C during the period of extensive instrumental measurements, which began in the late 1800s. Most of the warming, about 0.5 degree C, occurred after 1950. The causes of observed warming can be investigated best for the past 50 years, because most climate forcings were observed then, especially since satellite measurements of the sun, stratospheric aerosols and ozone began in the 1970s. Furthermore, 70 percent of the anthropogenic increase of greenhouse gases occurred after 1950.

The most important quantity is the planetary energy imbalance [*see box on page 52*]. This imbalance is a consequence of the long time that it takes the ocean to warm. We conclude that the earth is now out of balance by something between 0.5 and one watt per square meter—that much more solar radiation is being absorbed by the earth than is being emitted as heat to space. Even if atmospheric composition does not change further, the earth's surface will therefore eventually warm another 0.4 to 0.7 degree C.

Most of the energy imbalance has been heat going into the ocean. Sydney Levitus of the National Oceanic and Atmospheric Administration has analyzed ocean temperature changes of the past 50 years, finding that the world ocean heat content increased about 10 watt-years per square meter in the past 50 years. He also finds that the rate of ocean heat storage in recent years is consistent with our estimate that the earth is now out of energy balance by 0.5 to one watt per square meter. Note that the amount of heat required

Earth's Energy Imbalance

The earth's energy is balanced when the outgoing heat from the earth equals the incoming energy from the sun. At present the energy budget is not balanced (*see diagram and table on page 53*). Human-made aerosols have increased reflection of sunlight by the earth, but this reflection is more than offset by the trapping of heat radiation by greenhouse gases. The excess energy—about one watt per square meter—warms the ocean and melts ice. The simulated planetary energy imbalance (*see graph on page 53*) is confirmed by measurements of heat stored in the oceans. The planetary energy imbalance is a critical metric, in that it measures the net climate forcing and foretells future global warming already in the pipeline.

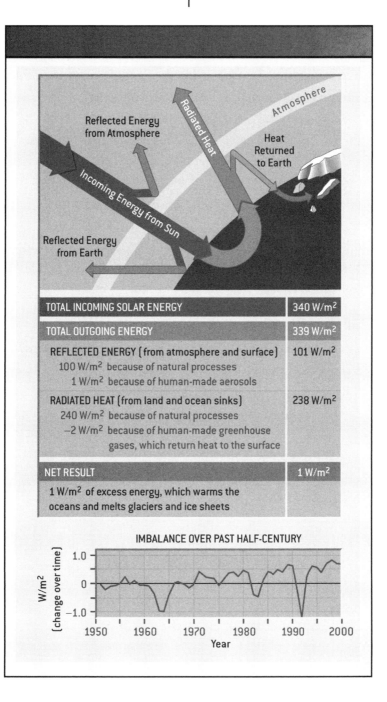

Reflected Energy
from Atmosphere

Atmosphere

Radiated Heat

Heat
Returned
to Earth

Incoming Energy from Sun

Reflected Energy
from Earth

TOTAL INCOMING SOLAR ENERGY	340 W/m²
TOTAL OUTGOING ENERGY	339 W/m²
REFLECTED ENERGY (from atmosphere and surface) 100 W/m² because of natural processes 1 W/m² because of human-made aerosols	101 W/m²
RADIATED HEAT (from land and ocean sinks) 240 W/m² because of natural processes −2 W/m² because of human-made greenhouse gases, which return heat to the surface	238 W/m²
NET RESULT	1 W/m²
1 W/m² of excess energy, which warms the oceans and melts glaciers and ice sheets	

IMBALANCE OVER PAST HALF-CENTURY

W/m²
(change over time)

to melt enough ice to raise sea level one meter is about 12 watt-years (averaged over the planet), energy that could be accumulated in 12 years if the planet is out of balance by one watt per square meter.

The agreement with observations, for both the modeled temperature change and ocean heat storage, leaves no doubt that observed global climate change is being driven by natural and anthropogenic forcings. The current rate of ocean heat storage is a critical planetary metric: it not only determines the amount of additional global warming already in the pipeline, but it also equals the reduction in climate forcings needed to stabilize the earth's present climate.

The Time Bomb

The goal of the United Nations Framework Convention on Climate Change, produced in Rio de Janeiro in 1989, is to stabilize atmospheric composition to "prevent dangerous anthropogenic interference with the climate system" and to achieve that goal in ways that do not disrupt the global economy. Defining the level of warming that constitutes "dangerous anthropogenic interference" is thus a crucial but difficult part of the problem.

The U.N. established an Intergovernmental Panel on Climate Change (IPCC) with responsibility for analysis of global warming. The IPCC has defined climate-forcing scenarios, used these for simulations of 21st-century climate, and estimated the impact of temperature and precipitation changes on agriculture, natural ecosystems, wildlife and other matters. The IPCC estimates sea-level change as large as several tens of centimeters in 100 years, if global warming reaches several degrees Celsius. The group's calculated sea-level

Climate Forcings

A climate forcing is a mechanism that alters the global energy balance. A forcing can be natural––fluctuations in the earth's orbit, for example––or human-made, such as aerosols and greenhouse gases. Human-made climate forcings now dominate natural forcings. Carbon dioxide is the largest forcing, but air pollutants (black carbon, ozone, methane) together are comparable. (Aerosol effects are not known accurately.)

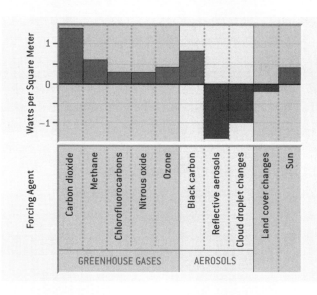

change is due mainly to thermal expansion of ocean water, with little change in ice-sheet volume.

These moderate climate effects, even with rapidly increasing greenhouse gases, leave the impression that we are not close to dangerous anthropogenic interference. I will argue, however, that we are much closer than is generally realized, and thus the emphasis should be on mitigating the changes rather than just adapting to them.

The dominant issue in global warming, in my opinion, is sea-level change and the question of how fast ice sheets can disintegrate. A large portion of the world's people live within a few meters of sea level, with trillions of dollars of infrastructure. The need to preserve global coastlines sets a low ceiling on the level of global warming that would constitute dangerous anthropogenic interference.

The history of the earth and the present human-made planetary energy imbalance together paint a disturbing picture about prospects for sea-level change. Data from the Antarctic temperature record show that the warming of the past 50 years has taken global temperature back to approximately the peak of the current interglacial (the Holocene). There is some additional warming in the pipeline that will take us about halfway to the highest global temperature level of the previous interglacial (the Eemian), which was warmer than the Holocene, with sea level estimated to have been five to six meters higher. One additional watt per square meter of forcing, over and above that today, will take global temperature approximately to the maximum level of the Eemian.

The main issue is: How fast will ice sheets respond to global warming? The IPCC calculates only a slight change in the ice sheets in 100 years; however, the IPCC calculations include only the gradual effects of changes in snowfall, evaporation and melting. In the real world, ice-sheet disintegration is driven by highly nonlinear processes and feedbacks. The peak rate of deglaciation following the last ice age was a sustained rate of melting of more than 14,000 cubic kilometers a year—about one meter of sea level rise every 20 years, which was maintained for several centuries. This period of most rapid melt coincided, as well as can be measured, with the time of most rapid warming.

Given the present unusual global warming rate on an already warm planet, we can anticipate that areas with summer melt and rain will expand over larger areas of Greenland and fringes of Antarctica. Rising sea level itself tends to lift marine ice shelves that buttress land ice, unhinging them from anchor points. As ice shelves break up, this accelerates movement of land ice to the ocean. Although building of glaciers is slow, once an ice sheet begins to collapse, its demise can be spectacularly rapid.

The human-induced planetary energy imbalance provides an ample supply of energy for melting ice. Furthermore, this energy source is supplemented by increased absorption of sunlight by ice sheets darkened by black-carbon aerosols, and the positive feedback process as meltwater darkens the ice surface.

These considerations do not mean that we should expect large sea-level change in the next few years. Preconditioning of ice sheets for accelerated breakup may require a long time, perhaps many centuries. (The satellite ICESat, recently launched by NASA, may be able to detect early signs of accelerating ice-sheet breakup.) Yet I suspect that significant sea-level rise could begin much sooner if the planetary energy imbalance continues to increase. It seems clear that global warming beyond some limit will make a large sea-level change inevitable for future generations. And once large-scale ice-sheet breakup is under way, it will be impractical to stop. Dikes may protect limited regions, such as Manhattan and the Netherlands, but most of the global coastlines will be inundated.

I argue that the level of dangerous anthropogenic influence is likely to be set by the global temperature and planetary radiation imbalance at which substantial deglaciation becomes practically impossible to avoid. Based on the paleoclimate evidence, I suggest that the highest prudent level of additional global warming is not more than about one degree C. This means that additional climate forcing should not exceed about one watt per square meter.

Climate-Forcing Scenarios

The IPCC defines many climate-forcing scenarios for the 21st century based on multifarious "story lines" for population growth, economic development and energy sources. It estimates that added climate forcing in the next 50 years is one to three watts per square meter for carbon dioxide and two to four watts per square meter with other gases and aerosols included. Even the IPCC's minimum added forcing would cause dangerous anthropogenic interference with the climate system based on our criterion.

The IPCC scenarios may be unduly pessimistic, however. First, they ignore changes in emissions, some already under way, because of concerns about global warming. Second, they assume that true air pollution will continue to get worse, with ozone, methane and black carbon all greater in 2050 than in 2000. Third, they give short shrift to technology advances that can reduce emissions in the next 50 years.

An alternative way to define scenarios is to examine current trends of climate-forcing agents, to ask why they are changing as observed, and to try to understand whether reasonable actions could encourage further changes in the growth rates.

The growth rate of the greenhouse-gas climate forcing peaked in the early 1980s at almost 0.5 watt per square meter per decade but declined by the 1990s to about 0.3 watt per square meter per decade. The primary reason for the decline was reduced emissions of chloro-fluorocarbons, whose production was phased out because of their destructive effect on stratospheric ozone.

The two most important greenhouse gases, with chlorofluorocarbons on the decline, are carbon dioxide and methane. The growth rate of carbon dioxide surged after World War II, flattened out from the mid-1970s to the mid-1990s, and rose moderately in recent years to the current growth rate of about two parts per million per year. The methane growth rate has declined dramatically in the past 20 years, by at least two thirds.

These growth rates are related to the rate of global fossil-fuel use. Fossil-fuel emissions increased by more than 4 percent a year from the end of World War II until 1975 but subsequently by only about 1 percent a year. The change in fossil-fuel growth rate occurred after the oil embargo and price increases of the 1970s, with subsequent emphasis on energy efficiency. Methane growth has also been affected by other factors, including changes in rice farming and increased efforts to capture methane at landfills and in mining operations.

If recent growth rates of these greenhouse gases continued, the added climate forcing in the next 50 years would be about 1.5 watts per square meter. To this must be added the change caused by other forcings, such as atmospheric ozone and aerosols. These forcings are not well monitored globally, but it is known that they are increasing in some countries while decreasing in others. Their net effect should be small, but it could add as much as 0.5 watt per square meter. Thus, if there is no slowing of emission rates, the human-made climate forcing could increase by two watts per square meter in the next 50 years.

This "current trends" growth rate of climate forcings is at the low end of the IPCC range of two to four watts per square meter. The IPCC four watts per square meter scenario requires 4 percent a year exponential growth of carbon dioxide emissions maintained for 50 years and large growth of air pollution; it is implausible.

Nevertheless, the "current trends" scenario is larger than the one watt per square meter level that I suggested as our current best estimate for the level of dangerous anthropogenic influence. This raises the question of whether there is a feasible scenario with still lower climate forcing.

A Brighter Future

I have developed a specific alternative scenario that keeps added climate forcing in the next 50 years at about one watt per square meter. It has two components: first, halt or reverse growth of air pollutants, specifically soot, atmospheric ozone and methane; second, keep average fossil-fuel carbon dioxide emissions in the next 50 years about the same as today. The carbon dioxide and non–carbon dioxide portions of the scenario are equally important. I argue that they are feasible and at the same time protect human health and increase agricultural productivity.

In addressing air pollution, we should emphasize the constituents that contribute most to global warming. Methane offers a great opportunity. If human sources of methane are reduced, it may even be possible to get the atmospheric methane amount to decline, thus providing a cooling that would partially offset the carbon dioxide increase. Reductions of black-carbon aerosols would help counter the warming effect of reductions in sulfate aerosols. Atmospheric ozone precursors, besides methane, especially nitrogen oxides and volatile organic compounds, must be reduced to decrease low-level atmospheric ozone, the prime component of smog.

Actions needed to reduce methane, such as methane capture at landfills and at waste management facilities and during the mining of fossil fuels, have economic benefits that partially offset the costs. In some cases, methane's value as a fuel entirely pays for the cost of capture. Reducing black carbon would also have economic benefits, both in the decreased loss of life and work-years (minuscule soot particles carry toxic organic compounds and metals deep into lungs) and in increased agricultural productivity in certain parts of the world. Prime sources of black carbon are diesel fuels and biofuels (wood and cow dung, for example).

But What About . . .

"Last winter was so cold! I don't notice any global warming!"
Global warming is ubiquitous, but its magnitude so far is only about one degree Fahrenheit. Day-to-day weather fluctuations are roughly 10 degrees F. Even averaged over a season this natural year-to-year variability is about two degrees F, so global warming does not make every season warmer than a few decades ago. But global warming already makes the probability of a warmer

than "normal" season about 60 percent, rather than the 30 percent that prevailed from 1950 to 1980.

"The warming of the past century is just a natural rebound from the little ice age."
Any rebound from the European little ice age, which peaked in 1650–1750, would have been largely complete by the 20th century. Indeed, the natural long-term climate trend today would be toward a colder climate were it not for human activities.

"Isn't human-made global warming saving us from the next ice age?"
Yes, but the gases that we have added to the atmosphere are already far more than needed for that purpose.

"The surface warming is mainly urban 'heat island' effects near weather stations."
Not so. As predicted, the greatest warming is found in remote regions such as central Asia and Alaska. The largest areas of surface warming are over the ocean, far from urban locations (see maps at www.giss.nasa.gov/data/update/gistemp [note: this link is now automatically forwarded to http://data.giss.nasa.gov/gistemp/]). Temperature profiles in the solid earth, at hundreds of boreholes around the world, imply a warming of the continental surfaces between 0.5 and one degree C in the past century.

Reducing Emissions

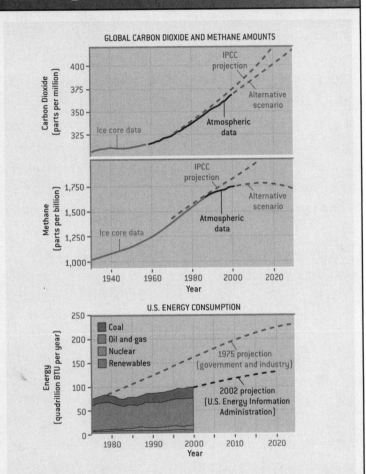

GLOBAL CARBON DIOXIDE AND METHANE AMOUNTS

U.S. ENERGY CONSUMPTION

Observed amounts of carbon dioxide and methane (*top two graphs*) fall below IPCC estimates, which have proved consistently pessimistic. Although the author's alternative scenario agrees better with observations, continuation on that path requires a gradual slowdown in carbon dioxide and methane emissions. Improvements in energy efficiency (*bottom graph on page 64*) have allowed energy use in the U.S. to fall below projections in recent decades, but more rapid efficiency gains are needed to achieve the carbon dioxide emissions of the alternative scenario, unless nuclear power and renewable energies grow substantially.

These sources need to be dealt with for health reasons. Diesel could be burned more cleanly with improved technologies; however, there may be even better solutions, such as hydrogen fuel, which would eliminate ozone precursors as well as soot.

Improved energy efficiency and increased use of renewable energies might level carbon dioxide emissions in the near term. Long-term reduction of carbon dioxide emissions is a greater challenge, as energy use will continue to rise. Progress is needed across the board: continued efficiency improvements, more renewable energy, and new technologies that produce little or no carbon dioxide or that capture and sequester it. Next-generation nuclear power, if acceptable to the public, could be an important contributor. There may be new technologies before 2050 that we have not imagined.

Observed global carbon dioxide and methane trends [*see box on page 64*] for the past several years show that the real world is falling below all IPCC scenarios. It remains to be proved whether the smaller observed growth rates are a fluke, soon to return to IPCC rates, or are a meaningful difference. In contrast, the projections of my alternative scenario and the observed growth rates are in agreement. This is not surprising, because that scenario was defined with observations in mind. And in the three years since the alternative scenario was defined, observations have continued on that path. I am not suggesting, however, that the alternative scenario can be achieved without concerted efforts to reduce anthropogenic climate forcings.

How can I be optimistic if climate is closer to the level of dangerous anthropogenic interference than has been realized? If we compare the situation today with that 10 to 15 years ago, we note that the main elements required to halt climate change have come into being with remarkable rapidity. I realize that it will not be easy to stabilize greenhouse-gas concentrations, but I am optimistic because I expect that empirical evidence for climate change and its impacts will continue to accumulate and that this will influence the public, public-interest groups, industry and governments at various levels. The question is: Will we act soon enough?

The Author

James Hansen is director of the NASA Goddard Institute for Space Studies and a researcher at the Columbia University Earth Institute. He received his Ph.D. in physics and astronomy from the University of Iowa, where he studied under James Van Allen. Hansen is best known for his testimony to congressional committees in the 1980s that helped to raise awareness of the global warming issue.

The air surrounding Earth is polluted with chloro-fluorocarbons (CFCs). CFCs are human-made chemicals that have no known effect on humans or other life-forms. They were first created in the 1930s and widely used for fifty years in refrigerators and aerosol cans. Not until 1974 did scientists realize that they may be harming the environment.

This article is about Mario Molina, one of the scientists who first suggested CFCs could be destroying the ozone layer, the natural shield that protects the planet from solar radiation. Since this suggestion, his theory was confirmed when a thinning ozone layer was discovered over the South Pole in 1985. As a result of this discovery, twenty-seven nations signed the Montreal Protocol in 1987, agreeing to reduce or ban the use of CFCs. Later revisions to the Montreal Protocol brought almost 189 nations to the table to sign the agreement.

Shortly after CFCs were reduced or banned, scientists found that the rate at which the ozone was disappearing actually slowed. In this case, a *harmful air pollutant was detected early and effectively banned worldwide—a rare success story for the environment.* —KW

"Profile: Mario Molina"
by Sasha Nemecek
Scientific American, **November 1997**

Mario Molina is walking me through his laboratory at the Massachusetts Institute of Technology, which is overflowing with exotic equipment. He makes his way to a small room in the back of the lab where he points out one of his latest toys, a powerful microscope hooked up to a video camera. He details how he and his students designed this high-tech setup to watch the formation of cloud particles. Despite his enthusiastic description, my mind wanders—I'm distracted by the dazzling clouds visible (without magnification) through the large window over Molina's shoulder. Somehow I did not expect that the man who suggested that chlorofluoro-carbons (CFCs) were destroying the ozone layer, some 20 kilometers above our heads, would use a microscope to probe the vast expanses of the atmosphere.

But within the confines of his laboratory, the Nobel Prize–winning Molina has seen quite a bit—much of it troubling. Molina is not an alarmist by temperament: "I've never claimed the world was coming to an end," he chuckles, yet a hint of seriousness remains in his gentle voice. When Molina and his colleague F. Sherwood Rowland of the University of California at Irvine announced their CFC findings in 1974, it seemed to many people that, in fact, the sky was falling.

Damage to the protective ozone layer, which shields the earth's surface from harmful ultraviolet radiation, would mean outbreaks of skin cancer and cataracts as well as the loss of crops and wildlife. So great was the concern that 10 years ago this fall, governments around the globe outlawed CFCs by signing the Montreal Protocol on Substances That Deplete the Ozone Layer.

The reluctant Cassandra of the chemistry world started out just having fun. As a young boy, he showed an interest in chemistry, so his indulgent parents allowed him to convert one bathroom in the spacious family home in Mexico City into a private laboratory.

After boarding school in Switzerland and graduate schools in Germany and France, Molina made his way to the University of California at Berkeley to complete his Ph.D. in physical chemistry. When he arrived in 1968, the campus was embroiled in student unrest about the Vietnam War. His time at Berkeley served as an awakening for him about the significance of science and technology to society. (Molina's time there had a personal significance as well: fellow graduate student Luisa Tan would later become his wife and frequent research collaborator.) Molina's project was rather academic: using lasers to study how molecules behave during chemical reactions. But because laser technology also can be used in weapons, the work was unpopular with student activists.

"We had to think of these issues: Why are we doing what we are doing? Would the resources be better spent in some other way? Is science good or bad?" Molina asks, waxing philosophical. "I came to the conclusion that science itself is neither good nor bad." Technology—what people do with science—was another story.

A desire to understand the implications of technology led Molina to study CFCs during a postdoctoral fellowship under Rowland. "All we knew is that these industrial compounds were unusually stable. We could measure them everywhere in the atmosphere," Molina says. "We wondered: What happens to them? Should we worry?"

The irony of CFCs is that years ago they were initially valued precisely because there seemed to be no need to worry. At a 1930 meeting the inventor of the compounds inhaled CFC vapors and then blew out a candle to show that the chemicals were neither toxic nor flammable. Over the next 50 years, CFCs made an array of new technologies possible: modern refrigerators, household and automobile air conditioners, aerosol spray cans, Styrofoam, cleaning techniques for microchips and other electronic parts.

Most emissions, such as exhaust from cars and smokestacks, actually never get very high in the air— the pollutants react with the hydroxyl radical (OH), which is essentially an atmospheric detergent that makes compounds soluble in rainwater. Molina checked to see how fast CFCs would react with hydroxyl radicals. The answer: zip. "It seemed that maybe nothing whatsoever interesting would happen to them," he says.

If chemicals could not break down CFCs, perhaps sunlight would. Based on their laboratory observations, Rowland and Molina realized that in the stratosphere, ultraviolet radiation is sufficiently energetic to break apart CFC molecules, releasing, among other substances, highly reactive chlorine atoms. Small amounts of chlorine can destroy ozone by acting as a catalyst (that is, the chlorine is not used up in the process of breaking down ozone).

In June 1974 Rowland and Molina published their paper in the journal *Nature* proposing a connection between CFCs and destruction of the ozone layer. Much to their surprise, the article received little notice. A few months later the two held a press conference at a chemistry meeting. "Eventually, we caught people's attention," Molina says.

Indeed. Over the next few years, letters about CFCs poured into Congress—the final tally is second only to the number received about the Vietnam War. The government responded quickly, passing amendments to the Clean Air Act in 1977 that called for the regulation of any substance "reasonably anticipated to affect the stratosphere." Soon the use of CFCs as propellants in spray cans was banned in the U.S. Chemical companies began to seek alternatives to CFCs; compounds known as hydrochlorofluorocarbons (HCFCs) and hydrofluoro-carbons (HFCs) are the most common choices. (Although HCFCs still contribute to ozone depletion because they contain chlorine, they are not as hazardous as CFCs, because they typically fall apart before reaching the stratosphere. The HFCs pose no threat to the ozone layer.)

Significantly, this flurry of action took place despite the fact that no one had ever observed any loss of stratospheric ozone. The famous hole in the ozone layer above Antarctica was not even detected until 1985. Molina commends this "important precedent in the use of precautionary principles" and suggests that the need to "do something even though the evidence is not there [is] very typical of environmental issues."

A more comprehensive international treaty regulating CFCs took longer to negotiate. But in September 1987 more than two dozen countries signed the Montreal Protocol. The agreement imposed an immediate reduction in the production and use of CFCs; subsequent amendments led to a total phaseout of CFCs in developed countries in 1995 (developing countries have until 2010).

Although the Montreal Protocol was signed after the discovery of the Antarctic ozone hole, many scientists and policymakers at the time were still unsure whether the ozone hole had been caused by CFCs or whether it was just part of a natural cycle. Molina himself remembers that when he first heard news of the ozone hole he "had no idea" whether CFCs were truly to blame. To prove the connection between CFCs and the Antarctic ozone hole, Molina and his

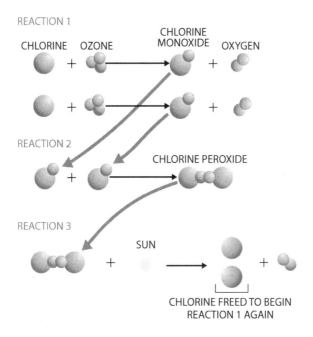

REACTION 1

CHLORINE   OZONE   CHLORINE MONOXIDE   OXYGEN

REACTION 2

CHLORINE PEROXIDE

REACTION 3

SUN

CHLORINE FREED TO BEGIN
REACTION 1 AGAIN

Chlorine destroys ozone but is not consumed in the process. Mario and Luisa T. Molina proposed this series of reactions to explain how CFCs caused the Antarctic ozone hole.

wife proposed a new series of chemical reactions in 1987 that measurements confirmed in 1991.

That satisfied most science and policy experts, although a few critics still persist. As late as 1995 (ironically, the same year Molina won the Nobel Prize for Chemistry, along with Rowland and Paul J. Crutzen of the Max Planck Institute for Chemistry in Mainz, Germany), Congress held hearings questioning whether the ozone hole was real and, if so, whether CFCs were really the culprit. The state of Arizona declared the Montreal Protocol invalid within its boundaries. Molina's patience is clearly tried by these suggestions. "You can go to the stratosphere and see how much chlorine there is and convince yourself that it's coming from CFCs," he says, his voice rising.

In the scientific community, the ozone problem is basically settled. Today the challenges lie more in the area of enforcing the Montreal Protocol. (The latest concern: a burgeoning black market in CFC trade.) Molina and his research group have moved on as well, investigating a wide range of reactions that occur in the atmosphere, including some that are important in urban air pollution. And Molina now spends less time in the lab and more time speaking to government officials on policy questions. In 1994 President Bill Clinton appointed him a science and technology adviser to the administration.

Molina also encourages students from developing countries, particularly in Latin America, to study environmental sciences. (He is the first Mexican-American to win a Nobel Prize and the first person born in Mexico to win in the sciences.) Part of his prize money has gone to create a fellowship for these students to study in the U.S. Given the environmental problems faced by developing nations, including deforestation, desertification, and worsening water and air pollution, Molina considers it crucial to involve people from these regions when crafting solutions.

Molina's smog-choked hometown offers a poignant tale. "When I was a kid in Mexico City, [pollution] was not a problem," he recalls. Over the past 50 years, of course, that has changed. Molina finds it puzzling that more is not done to combat pollution in cities, which is so plainly obvious compared with CFC pollution in the stratosphere. "You can already see it and smell it and breathe it," he comments.

Molina hopes this argument will convince policymakers, specifically in the developing world, to reduce emissions of fossil fuels now, a move that should also help alleviate global warming. Although Molina sees the evidence linking fossil fuels and climate change as still somewhat tentative, the connection between fossil fuels and urban pollution is unequivocal—and thereby on much firmer footing than the CFC-ozone depletion connection was when controls on CFCs were established. "If we take a look at the whole picture, it is much clearer to me that some strong action needs to be taken on the energy issue." Interesting what shows up in Molina's microscope.

2 Water

Water resources in small countries are often polluted by human waste. This is because few people have modern plumbing or running water— so waste is collected in outhouses and then either seeps into groundwater or gets emptied into nearby rivers.

Water sanitation is the number one priority in many of these countries, but installing modern plumbing is not always an option. In South Africa, for example, there is very little water to use for plumbing and very little money to build plumbing systems. Instead, scientists suggest dumping waste into ponds populated with algae that can naturally remove toxins from human waste. This process is cheap, uses little water, and leaves behind dead algae that can be dried and used as fertilizer or fish food.

The following article is about the work of one scientist, Peter D. Rose, currently the director of the Environmental Biotechnology Research Unit at Rhodes University in Grahamstown, South Africa. Since this article was published in 1995, Rose has continued his work using algae to clean up wastewater. He and his colleagues have constructed full-scale plants to test the science, and it appears to be working. —KW

"Sewage Treatment Plants"
by W. Wayt Gibbs
Scientific American, November 1995

Andile Tiyani wrinkles his nose in distaste as he points to a listing outhouse patched together from scraps of wood and corrugated metal. The tiny shack, huddled among thousands of other slightly larger shacks that house the black residents of the Crossroads township outside of Cape Town, South Africa, is just large enough to accommodate a toilet seat mounted over a bucket. The bucket is overflowing.

"In better areas, they periodically take these buckets to the edge of town and dump them," Tiyani explains. "When the rains come, it all runs into the streams, where people wash their clothes, and it contaminates the groundwater, which lies just four meters below the surface here." In five neighboring townships, home to some one million black South Africans, conditions vary only slightly. In Harare, residents share pit toilets. Tiyani's house in the middle-class district of Guguletu is among the most hygienic around, sporting a septic tank.

Bringing basic sanitation services to the millions who lack them is a top public health priority for the new South African government. It is also a huge fiscal challenge. As in so many other poor countries, expensive Western technologies are simply not an option.

One cheap Western technology may be, though. Nearly 500 miles to the east of Cape Town, Peter D. Rose of Rhodes University is adapting an American algae-based system to meet the needs of sub-Saharan Africa. In a nearby pilot plant, due to be completed next year, the waste of 500 to 1,000 people will be pumped through 1,000 square meters of ponds and raceways full of *Spirulina*, a single-celled plant that thrives on salty, nutrient-rich sewage. Exposed to sunlight and stirred gently, algae ingest most of the waste. A small remainder of heavy metals and other inorganic detritus sinks to the bottom of the pits.

Ponds replete with algae have been used to treat waste for at least a century. But it is only in the past decade that advanced algal systems, in which just certain species are actively cultivated, have begun to challenge the activated-sludge techniques commonly used in industrial nations.

Advanced algal ponding processes now offer several advantages, says William J. Oswald of the University of California at Berkeley, who has worked on the technology since the 1950s. The equipment and power used in conventional plants to mix incoming sewage with pressurized air and bacteria-rich sludge are avoided in algal systems, so the latter cost about one half as much to build and operate. They can run on less water—important in arid climes such as South Africa's.

They produce far less sludge, which is generally trucked to landfills or dumped at sea. In fact, the main product is tons upon tons of dead algae, which when dried makes a good fertilizer or additive for fish food. And because the plants produce lots of oxygen, they don't stink. "We had a wine tasting not long ago at the [algal pond] plant in St. Helena," which processes 500,000 gallons of sewage a day in the heart of California wine country. "It was very picturesque," Oswald says.

For Rose, the technology holds a dual attraction. The potential for improving community sanitation throughout the Third World is obvious. (Researchers in Kuwait and Morocco are also running tests.) "But it has allowed us to do some very interesting fundamental research as well," Rose says, donning his biochemist's cap. As South African science budgets are increasingly squeezed by a government facing more urgent needs, many scientists there are scrambling to find relevant applications to justify their basic research.

"One of the future benefits of the process is that once you have this algal biomass, you might be able to engineer it to produce by-products that are more valuable than just animal feed," Rose continues. His team recently elucidated the biochemical mechanism by which another algae, *Dunaliella salina*, produces massive amounts of beta carotene (the nutrient used by the body to make vitamin A) when stressed by excessive salt or heat.

Rose has also demonstrated that *Spirulina* ponds can treat industrial waste, particularly from tanneries. "The tanning industry is set to explode in Africa," says Randall Hepburn, Rhodes's dean of science. "The reason is simple: we kill 650 million sheep, goats, pigs and cows each year. But the hides of all but 3 percent of those are left to rot. That is going to change."

The possibility of a tanning boom worries some African environmentalists. "Tanneries produce some of the worst effluents of any industry: sulfides, ammonia, heavy metals," Rose says. "It's shocking stuff." So he was a bit surprised several years ago when he noticed giant blooms of *Spirulina* forming in a tannery's evaporation pond. The discovery has led to test projects at tanneries near Cape Town, in Namibia and in the Transvaal, where algal treatment systems are successfully—and inexpensively—squelching odors and reclaiming water that was previously wasted through evaporation.

"Rapid industrialization in Third World countries is very often done at the expense of the environment, because the costs of First World remediation technologies cannot be afforded simultaneously," Rose says. "To come up with a low-cost method that turns waste into something not only safe but useful—well, that's the first prize in biotechnology."

Having water available to irrigate crops is becoming rare in many parts of the world. Irrigation is the practice of routing water to nourish farmland (instead of just depending on natural rainfall). For centuries, humans have diverted rivers and constructed pipelines to water crops and produce food. According to Sandra Postel, author of the following article, irrigation accounts for two-thirds of the water used throughout the world today.

As human populations grow and more food is needed to feed the additional people, irrigation practices will require more and more water. In countries already stressed for water, populations are expected to grow from 500 million to 3 billion over the next twenty-five years. This increase in population means we will need to grow more food.

But where will the water needed to grow more food come from? This article suggests we won't be able to find or create any extra water, so we will need to use the water we have for irrigation more efficiently.

The author, who has studied freshwater issues for decades, recommends doing two things: using water more efficiently in large-scale agriculture and bringing low-cost technology to poor farmers so the water can be used smartly. —KW

"Growing More Food with Less Water"
by Sandra Postel
Scientific American, **February 2001**

Six thousand years ago farmers in Mesopotamia dug
a ditch to divert water from the Euphrates River.
With that successful effort to satisfy their thirsty
crops, they went on to form the world's first irrigation-
based civilization. This story of the ancient Sumerians
is well known. What is not so well known is that
Sumeria was one of the earliest civilizations to crumble
in part because of the consequences of irrigation.

Sumerian farmers harvested plentiful wheat and
barley crops for some 2,000 years thanks to the extra
water brought in from the river, but the soil eventually
succumbed to salinization—the toxic buildup of salts
and other impurities left behind when water evaporates.
Many historians argue that the poisoned soil, which
could not support sufficient food production, figured
prominently in the society's decline.

Far more people depend on irrigation in the modern
world than did in ancient Sumeria. About 40 percent
of the world's food now grows in irrigated soils, which
make up 18 percent of global cropland. Farmers who
irrigate can typically reap two or three harvests
every year *and* get higher crop yields. As a result, the
spread of irrigation has been a key factor behind the
near tripling of global grain production since 1950.
Done correctly, irrigation will continue to play a

leading role in feeding the world, but as history shows, dependence on irrigated agriculture also entails significant risks.

Today irrigation accounts for two thirds of water use worldwide and as much as 90 percent in many developing countries. Meeting the crop demands projected for 2025, when the planet's population is expected to reach eight billion, could require an additional 192 cubic miles of water—a volume nearly equivalent to the annual flow of the Nile 10 times over. No one yet knows how to supply that much additional water in a way that protects supplies for future use.

Severe water scarcity presents the single biggest threat to future food production. Even now many freshwater sources—underground aquifers and rivers—are stressed beyond their limits. As much as 8 percent of food crops grows on farms that use groundwater faster than the aquifers are replenished, and many large rivers are so heavily diverted that they don't reach the sea for much of the year. As the number of urban dwellers climbs to five billion by 2025, farmers will have to compete even more aggressively with cities and industry for shrinking resources.

Despite these challenges, agricultural specialists are counting on irrigated land to produce most of the additional food that will be needed worldwide. Better management of soil and water, along with creative cropping patterns, can boost production from cropland that is watered only by rainfall, but the heaviest burden will fall on irrigated land. To fulfill its potential, irrigated agriculture requires a thorough redesign organized around two primary goals: cut water demands of mainstream agriculture and bring low-cost irrigation to poor farmers.

Fortunately, a great deal of room exists for improving the productivity of water used in agriculture. A first line of attack is to increase irrigation efficiency. At present, most farmers irrigate their crops by flooding their fields or channeling the water down parallel furrows, relying on gravity to move the water across the land. The plants absorb only a small fraction of the water; the rest drains into rivers or aquifers, or evaporates. In many locations this practice not only wastes and pollutes water but also degrades the land through erosion, waterlogging and salinization. More efficient and environmentally sound technologies exist that could reduce water demand on farms by up to 50 percent.

Drip systems rank high among irrigation technologies with significant untapped potential. Unlike flooding techniques, drip systems enable farmers to deliver water directly to the plants' roots drop by drop, nearly eliminating waste. The water travels at low pressure through a network of perforated plastic tubing installed on or below the surface of the soil, and it emerges through small holes at a slow but steady pace. Because the plants enjoy an ideal moisture environment, drip irrigation usually offers the added bonus of higher crop yields. Studies in India, Israel, Jordan, Spain and the U.S. have shown time and again that drip irrigation reduces water use by 30 to 70 percent and increases crop yield by 20 to 90 percent compared with flooding methods.

Sprinklers can perform almost as well as drip methods when they are designed properly. Traditional high-pressure irrigation sprinklers spray water high into the air to cover as large a land area as possible. The problem is that the more time the water spends in the air, the more of it evaporates and blows off course before reaching the plants. In contrast, new low-energy sprinklers deliver water in small doses through nozzles positioned just above the ground. Numerous farmers in Texas who have installed such sprinklers have found that their plants absorb 90 to 95 percent of the water that leaves the sprinkler nozzle.

Despite these impressive payoffs, sprinklers service only 10 to 15 percent of the world's irrigated fields, and drip systems account for just over 1 percent. The higher costs of these technologies (relative to simple flooding methods) have been a barrier to their spread, but so has the prevalence of national water policies that discourage rather than foster efficient water use. Many governments have set very low prices for publicly supplied irrigation, leaving farmers with little motivation to invest in ways to conserve water or to improve efficiency. Most authorities have also failed to regulate groundwater pumping, even in regions where aquifers are overtapped. Farmers might be inclined to conserve their own water supplies if they could profit from selling the surplus, but a number of countries prohibit or discourage this practice.

Efforts aside from irrigation technologies can also help reduce agricultural demand for water. Much potential lies in scheduling the timing of irrigation to more precisely match plants' water needs. Measurements of climate factors such as temperature and precipitation can be fed into a computer that calculates how much water a typical plant is consuming. Farmers can use this figure to determine, quite accurately, when and how much to irrigate their particular crops throughout the growing season. A 1995 survey conducted by the University of California at Berkeley found that, on average, farmers in California who used this tool reduced water use by 13 percent and achieved an 8 percent increase in yield—a big gain in water productivity.

An obvious way to get more benefit out of water is to use it more than once. Some communities use recycled wastewater. Treated wastewater accounts for 30 percent of Israel's agricultural water supply, for instance, and this share is expected to climb to 80 percent by 2025. Developing new crop varieties offers potential as well. In the quest for higher yields, scientists have already exploited many of the most fruitful agronomic options for growing more food with the same amount of water. The hybrid wheat and rice varieties that spawned the green revolution, for example, were bred to allocate more of the plants' energy—and thus their water uptake—into edible grain. The widespread adoption of high-yielding and early-maturing rice varieties has led to a roughly threefold increase in the amount of rice harvested per unit of water consumed—a tremendous achievement. No strategy in sight—neither conventional breeding techniques nor genetic engineering—could repeat those gains on such a grand scale, but modest improvements are likely.

Yet another way to do more with less water is to reconfigure our diets. The typical North American diet, with its large share of animal products, requires twice as much water to produce as the less meat-intensive diets common in many Asian and some European countries. Eating lower on the food chain could allow the same volume of water to feed two Americans instead of one, with no loss in overall nutrition.

Reducing the water demands of mainstream agriculture is critical, but irrigation will never reach its potential to alleviate rural hunger and poverty without additional efforts. Among the world's approximately 800 million undernourished people are millions of poor farm families who could benefit dramatically from access to irrigation water or to technologies that enable them to use local water more productively.

Most of these people live in Asia and Africa, where long dry seasons make crop production difficult or impossible without irrigation. For them, conventional irrigation technologies are too expensive for their small plots, which typically encompass fewer than five acres. Even the least expensive motorized pumps that are made for tapping groundwater cost about $350, far out of reach for farmers earning barely that much in a year. Where affordable irrigation technologies have been made available, however, they have proved remarkably successful.

I traveled to Bangladesh in 1998 to see one of these successes firsthand. Torrential rains drench Bangladesh during the monsoon months, but the country receives very little precipitation the rest of the year. Many fields lie fallow during the dry season, even though groundwater lies less than 20 feet below the surface. Over the past 17 years a foot-operated device called a treadle pump has transformed much of this land into productive, year-round farms.

To an affluent Westerner, this pump resembles a StairMaster exercise machine and is operated in much the same way. The user pedals up and down on two long bamboo poles, or treadles, which in turn activate two steel cylinders. Suction pulls groundwater into the cylinders and then dispenses it into a channel in the field. Families I spoke with said they often treadled four to six hours a day to irrigate their rice paddies and vegetable plots. But the hard work paid off: not only were they no longer hungry during the dry season, but they had surplus vegetables to take to market.

Costing less than $35, the treadle pump has increased the average net income for these farmers— which is often as little as a dollar a day—by $100 a year. To date, Bangladeshi farmers have purchased some 1.2 million treadle pumps, raising the productivity of more than 600,000 acres of farmland. Manufactured and marketed locally, the pumps are injecting at least an additional $350 million a year into the Bangladeshi economy.

In other impoverished and waterscarce regions, poor farmers are reaping the benefits of newly designed lowcost drip and sprinkler systems. Beginning with a $5 bucket kit for home gardens, a spectrum of drip systems keyed to different income levels and farm sizes is now enabling farmers with limited access to water to irrigate their land efficiently. In 1998 I spoke with farmers in the lower Himalayas of northern India, where crops are grown on terraces and irrigated with a scarce communal water supply. They expected to double their planted area with the increased efficiency brought about by affordable drip systems.

Bringing these low-cost irrigation technologies into more widespread use requires the creation of local, private-sector supply chains—including manufacturers, retailers and installers—as well as special innovations in marketing. The treadle pump has succeeded in Bangladesh in part because local businesses manufactured and sold the product and marketing specialists reached out to poor farmers with creative techniques, including an open-air movie and village demonstrations. The challenge is great, but so is the potential payoff. Paul Polak, a pioneer in the field of low-cost irrigation and president of International Development Enterprises in Lakewood, Colo., believes a realistic goal for the next 15 years is to reduce the hunger and poverty of 150 million of the world's poorest rural people through the spread of affordable small-farm irrigation techniques. Such an accomplishment would boost net income among the rural poor by an estimated $3 billion a year.

Over the next quarter of a century the number of people living in waterstressed countries will climb from 500 million to three billion. New technologies can help farmers around the world supply food for the growing population while simultaneously protecting rivers, lakes and aquifers. But broader societal changes—including slower population growth and reduced consumption—will also be necessary. Beginning with Sumeria, history warns against complacency when it comes to our agricultural foundation. With so many threats to the sustainability and productivity of our modern irrigation base now evident, it is a lesson worth heeding.

The Author

Sandra Postel directs the Global Water Policy Project in Amherst, Mass., and is a visiting senior lecturer in environmental studies at Mount Holyoke College. She is also a senior fellow of the Worldwatch Institute, where she served as vice president for research from 1988 to 1994.

Water used in aquaculture, or fish farming, may or may not be a worthwhile use of this resource. Today, hundreds of species of fish, shellfish, and other marine life are raised on farms to provide food for humans. In theory, farming these creatures takes the fishing pressure off wild populations at sea. But in reality, the economic and environmental success of the industry is very hard to judge. One reason it's so hard to get a handle on aquaculture is because the industry varies so much. Farms can be large or small, they can be located in the oceans or inland, and they can use many types of equipment to raise different species.

The following five articles focus on two marine animals commonly raised on farms: shrimp and salmon. On the shrimp side, environmentalists worry most about farms destroying the mangroves that often grow near the farms. Mangroves are widespread saltwater plants valued because they filter extra nutrients from the water and provide homes for small fish. On the salmon side, environmentalists worry most about farms polluting seawater (by loading the water with fish waste and extra nutrients) and farmed fish affecting wild populations (with farm diseases or interbreeding). The judgment on aquaculture's impact on water resources is still out, and the industry continues to grow. —KW

"The Promise and Perils of Aquaculture"
by the Editors
Scientific American Presents: The Oceans, Fall 1998

Aquaculture, or fish farming as it is often called,
might appear to be the perfect solution to the dire
problems facing many overly exploited varieties of
marine fauna. If people can raise enough fish on
farms, it stands to reason that they will be less inclined
to hunt them from the sea. So the phenomenal growth
of aquaculture in recent years might take some of the
pressure off wild populations. Unfortunately, this
seemingly logical supposition is surprisingly hard to
confirm.

The complication is that aquaculture often exploits
wild populations indirectly. Many of the species raised
on farms are fed fish meal produced from capture
fisheries. And countless farming operations rear

Commonly Raised Species

Fish

Asian seabass (*Lates calcarifer*)
Atlantic salmon (*Salmo salar*)
Atlantic cod (*Gadus morhua*)
Ayu sweetfish (*Plecoglossus altivelis*)
Bagrid catfish (*Chrysichthys nigrodigitatus*)
Bastard halibut (*Paralichthys olivaceus*)

Bluefish (*Pomatomus saltatrix*)
Cachama blanca (*Piaractus brachypomus*)
Channel catfish (*Ictalurus punctatus*)
Climbing perch (*Anabas testudineus*)
Common sole (*Solea vulgaris*)
European seabass (*Dicentrarchus labrax*)
Flathead gray mullet (*Mugil cephalus*)
Giant gourami (*Osphronemus goramy*)
Greasy grouper (*Epinephelus tauvina*)
Japanese eel (*Anguilla japonica*)
Japanese jack mackerel (*Trachurus japonicus*)
Kissing gourami (*Helostoma temmincki*)
Largemouth black bass (*Micropterus salmoides*)
Mangrove red snapper (*Lutjanus argentimaculatus*)
Milkfish (*Chanos chanos*)
Nile tilapia (*Oreochromis niloticus*)
North African catfish (*Clarias gariepinus*)
Northern pike (*Esox lucius*)
Pangas catfish (*Pangasius pangasius*)
Pike-perch (*Stizostedion lucioperca*)
Red seabream (*Pagrus major*)
Silver carp (*Hypophthalmichthys molitrix*)
Southern bluefin tuna (*Thunnus maccoyii*)
Snakeskin gourami (*Trichogaster pectoralis*)
Starry sturgeon (*Acipenser stellatus*)
Striped snakehead (*Channa striata*)
Turbot (*Psetta maxima*)

continued on following page

continued from previous page

CRUSTACEANS

American lobster (*Homarus americanus*)
Chinese river crab (*Eriocheir sinensis*)
Danube crayfish (*Astacus leptodactylus*)
European lobster (*Homarus gammarus*)
Giant tiger prawn (*Peneaus monodon*)
Giant river prawn (*Macrobrachium rosenbergii*)
Indo-Pacific swamp crab (*Scylla serrata*)
Longlegged spiny lobster (*Panulirus longipes*)
Red swamp crawfish (*Procambarus clarkii*)
Whiteleg shrimp (*Peneaus vannamei*)
Yabby crayfish (*Cherax destructor*)

MOLLUSKS

Blood cockle (*Anadara granosa*)
Blue mussel (*Mytilus edulis*)
Common edible cockle (*Cerastoderma edule*)
European abalone (*Haliotis tuberculata*)
Giant clam (*Tridacna gigas*)
Globose clam (*Mactra veneriformis*)
Japanese corbicula (*Corbicula japonica*)
Japanese pearl oyster (*Pinctada fucata*)
Northern quahog (*Mercenaria mercenaria*)
Pacific cupped oyster (*Crassostrea gigas*)
Pacific geoduck (*Panopea abrupta*)
Peruvian calico scallop (*Argopecten purpuratus*)
Pink conch (*Strombus gigas*)
Sand gaper (*Mya arenaria*)

juvenile fish taken from the ocean. For example, shrimp farmers in Latin America often shun larvae produced in hatcheries, because they believe that nature's shrimp are more robust. As a result, they will pay twice the price for captured larvae, and vast numbers of collectors take to shallow waters with fine mesh nets seeking them out. This intensive fishing constitutes a threat, but one is hard-pressed to demonstrate that it has actually diminished the numbers of wild shrimp.

Such uncertainty is one reason for the difficulty in weighing the benefits of aquaculture against its biological and environmental costs. Another stems from the very diversity of this industry. Farmers raise everything from fish to crustaceans, from mollusks to aquatic plants. In all, they produce in excess of 25 million metric tons every year of more than 260 different species. And these farmers employ many kinds of equipment in the process, including cages of netting suspended offshore, indoor tanks recirculating filtered water and open-air ponds flushed with seawater. So broad statements—both those that disparage and those that support the practice of aquaculture—rarely apply universally.

To illuminate some of the subtleties involved, the following four pages spotlight two common subjects of this industry—shrimp and salmon. Rearing such animals in captivity rather than fishing for them could help foster conservation. But making sure that these enterprises truly benefit wildlife remains a significant challenge for the future.

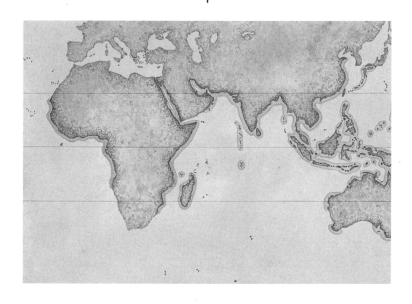

"Giant Questions about Shrimp"
by the Editors
Scientific American Presents: The Oceans, Fall 1998

The explosive growth of shrimp aquaculture in recent years has created worries about the environmental toll from this industry. One of the charges voiced by environmentalists is that the people constructing shallow ponds for shrimp farming all too often destroy mangroves, salt-tolerant trees that line the coast in much of the tropical world (*dark gray on map above*). These partially inundated mangrove forests filter excessive nutrients washed off the land before they reach the sea, and the submerged roots shelter a variety of creatures, including young fish. Although the destruction of mangroves also comes about for many reasons besides the construction of shrimp ponds, all these losses bode badly for the affected shores and ocean nearby. The essays here present two perspectives on this concern and other environmental problems arising from shrimp farming.

"Notes from an Adviser to the Shrimp Industry"
by Claude E. Boyd
Scientific American Presents: The Oceans, **Fall 1998**

It cannot be denied that a great deal of environmental damage has arisen from poor planning and management by shrimp farmers and lax government agencies in countries where this form of aquaculture is widespread. But shrimp farming is not always harmful to the environment. Unfortunately, some environmentalists have unfairly made sweeping condemnations of the entire industry.

One charge leveled against shrimp farming is that rich investors make quick profits and then abandon farms. Here the critics are just plain wrong. Although some shrimp farms have proved unsustainable and been abandoned, these farms usually were small, often consisting of only one or two cheaply constructed ponds, which were situated on unsuitable sites and operated without sufficient capital and expertise. Properly sited and well-constructed shrimp farms cost from $10,000 to $50,000 per hectare of pond and are expensive to operate. Such large investments cannot be recovered quickly, so owners want to make sure that their farms are productive for many years.

Shrimp farming is an interesting example of a situation in which a disproportionate amount of the environmental damage has resulted from smaller operators rather than from bigger ones. But it is possible for small-scale farmers to pool their resources in cooperatives or producer associations and greatly improve their management. Well-run operations require many workers up and down the line—for hatcheries, farms and processing plants—typically creating one or two jobs for each hectare of pond in production. Shrimp farming also stimulates local economies and provides import earnings for many developing nations.

So it would be a sad loss for many people if shrimp aquaculture disappeared. The trick is to manage these operations sensibly. Many shrimp farmers are, in fact, acutely aware of the damage that shrimp farming can do. They have learned that their long-term success depends on maintaining healthy conditions for their shrimp and that their prosperity is linked directly to environmental quality along nearby coasts. Degradation of the coastal zone makes aquaculture more difficult, so it is easy to convince most shrimp farmers that they have a vested interest in being good environmental stewards.

Several recent developments indicate that shrimp farmers are indeed moving toward environmentally friendly forms of production. The Australian Prawn Farmers Association established a formal code of practice for its members; the Association of Southeast Asian Nations Fisheries Network published a manual of good shrimp farm procedures; and the Food and Agriculture Organization of the United Nations presented technical guidelines for responsible fisheries that apply to shrimp farming. In addition, the Network of Aquaculture Centers in Asia-Pacific has created a detailed plan to improve the sustainability of aquaculture in general.

What is more, several recent scientific and trade meetings have focused on the connection between shrimp farming and the environment. Most countries now require environmental impact assessments for new shrimp farms. Thailand has instituted regulations in an effort to make sure that shrimp farmers adopt the best management practices possible. A particularly important development is the recent formation of the Global Aquaculture Alliance. This industry group is fostering responsible shrimp aquaculture, developing an elaborate code of practice and promoting consumer awareness with an "eco-label" for environmentally friendly shrimp.

Claude E. Boyd is a professor in the department of fisheries and allied aquaculture at Auburn University. He shares his expertise with shrimp farmers around the world through workshops and consulting tours.

"Comments from an Environmental Advocate"
by Jason W. Clay
Scientific American Presents: The Oceans, **Fall 1998**

Many businesspeople see natural resources as free for the taking. They count as costs only the labor and investment needed to extract them. There is no thought given to the cost of replacement or maintenance for the resources they use. Nowhere is this blindness more true than with shrimp aquaculturists, who often depend on access to public resources that, traditionally, have been used by many different groups.

Shrimp farmers must decide if they indeed want to address the environmental problems their industry has created. True, all economic activities have environmental consequences. Nevertheless, the goal of shrimp producers should be to reduce the deleterious effects on the environment as much as possible.

Some practices that would make shrimp farming more sustainable are already used by more progressive and well-financed shrimp producers. Around the world, however, there are hundreds of thousands of shrimp farmers. Each one makes decisions that affect his or her own future as well as those of others in this business. Shrimp aquaculture as it is conducted today in most parts of the world is not sustainable for very many decades into the future.

Perhaps an ideal, indefinitely sustainable system for shrimp farming is not possible, at least with current knowledge. Yet most shrimp farmers and others affected by this industry could agree that some practices are better than others, and the industry as a whole would benefit from the swift adoption of these improved techniques.

There are a number of business reasons to adopt more efficient and sustainable methods of shrimp production. For example, increasing the survival rates of young shrimp from less than 50 to 75 percent or more will reduce the initial outlays required for each crop. Similarly, more effective ways of feeding shrimp can reduce expenditures on food by a quarter to a half. These two simple changes would reduce the cost of cleaning effluents and moving ponds periodically. Ecuadorian shrimp farmers have been able to double their profits by such means.

Although other improvements may be more expensive, the boost to income in many instances will compensate for the required expenditures. Yet it is important to understand that some investments will not result in increased efficiency. These costs will have to be passed on to consumers, who are, after all, the ultimate polluters in the economic system. Regulations might bring increased prices. Or perhaps "green" shrimp will prove to command a premium from environmentally conscious consumers.

But producers who try to differentiate their product to gain market advantage must be able to prove their claims. People will pay more only if a reliable third party has verified assertions about the product being environmentally benign. Because there are no "name brands" of shrimp, such assurances will be difficult to judge.

Who should establish the guidelines for sustainable shrimp production? Today environmentalists, producers and some governments are each developing their own guidelines for sustainable shrimp aquaculture. But no single group, certainly not the producers themselves, will be able to create a credible system. Attaining that goal will require that these diverse groups agree on general principles, which can then be adapted to specific local conditions. Only through the adoption of such sustainable production systems will shrimp aquaculture be part of the solution for the next millennium rather than just another environmental problem that must be put right.

Jason W. Clay, a research fellow at the World Wildlife Fund in Washington, D.C., has taught at Harvard University. He has also worked for the U.S. Department of Agriculture and for Cultural Survival, a human-rights organization.

"Struggles with Salmon"
by Krista McKinsey
Scientific American Presents: The Oceans, Fall 1998

Producing almost 800,000 metric tons a year, salmon aquaculture has become a worldwide industry. Norway raises nearly half this tonnage, with Chile contributing 24 percent, Scotland 14 percent and British Columbia 4 percent. In all, aquaculture accounts for about a third of the salmon consumed annually. This now thriving industry burgeoned after wild stocks of salmon became too depleted to satisfy demand.

Populations of Atlantic salmon may have first begun to falter in the face of intensive fishing as early as the 1860s, and during the ensuing decades many fishers on both sides of the Atlantic moved to the western coast of North America to take advantage of the salmon there. Nevertheless, by the early 1970s, the numbers of Atlantic salmon had fallen sharply. The salmon fishery of the Pacific Northwest also proved fragile, essentially collapsing in 1994. Today in the U.S., only the Alaskan salmon fishery survives at a significant level.

To compensate for the failing production from capture fisheries, salmon farmers began setting up operations at coastal sites, beginning in Norway during the 1970s. These farmers learned to simulate the natural life cycle of wild salmon, which live most of their days in the ocean but lay their eggs in freshwater streams. The newly hatched fish typically spend up to a year meandering their way to the sea, where they migrate north to cold, nutrient-rich waters, allowing them to feed more easily. Three years later they return to breed in the same freshwater streams where they hatched. Although Pacific salmon die shortly after spawning, Atlantic salmon (the type used predominantly for aquaculture) can make the circuit twice.

On a farm, aquaculturists hatch eggs in freshwater and grow the fish for a year in tanks before transferring them to pens of netting suspended near shore in bays or estuaries. They feed the salmon pellets composed primarily of fish meal, vegetable matter and vitamins and, after three years, harvest and sell the fattened fish.

The success of salmon farms has been a boon for consumers, who have seen prices drop. But for others the results have been mixed. For example, some environmentalists are concerned about uneaten food and fish feces building up underneath densely stocked pens where currents are weak, resulting in a large deposit of nutrient-rich sediment on the seafloor. They fear that this sludge will overload bottom-dwelling organisms living in the vicinity.

Insufficient flushing may also foster the spread of disease among farmed salmon. This problem for farmers becomes an environmental concern if the salmon get loose. Fish can escape by accident during transport or through holes in faulty nets, and when released they are free to roam the oceans and coastlines. So disease-carrying salmon from farms could, at least in theory, pass pathogens to wild stocks.

On the western coast of North America, escaped Atlantic salmon can interact with the native Pacific species, and some people worry that the nonnative Atlantics could take over. Despite the large numbers involved (the government of British Columbia reported that more than 60,000 Atlantic salmon had slipped from their nets in 1994 and 1995 alone), thus far there is no evidence that Atlantic salmon pose any serious danger.

Robert R. Stickney, a fisheries researcher at Texas A&M University, points out that efforts to establish Atlantic salmon populations on the western coast began as early as the last century. Since then, there have been multiple attempts, but none were successful. Because those projects failed repeatedly, it is unlikely that renegade Atlantic salmon could pose a threat to the Pacific species. "It's a nonissue as long as you use the right fish," Stickney remarks. Atlantic salmon are good for farmers because they grow quickly and are more docile than the Pacific species, so the likelihood of them taking over local salmon runs is slim. William K. Hershberger of the Western Regional Aquaculture Center at the University of Washington agrees. "Results indicate that the competition with native fish is not a serious issue," he says, "but it is wise to continue monitoring the situation." John M. Epifanio, a geneticist with Trout Unlimited, a national nonprofit organization, is less optimistic. He notes that "the risk of displacing the native salmon is probably low." But he warns that "if the scale at which [salmon aquaculture] is happening is large enough, it'll happen eventually."

Another worry about the mass production of salmon arises because the densely populated pens tend to attract predators. Marine mammals and seabirds tear holes in the nets, releasing fish and swallowing profits. Farmers have tried everything from sonic devices to plastic whales to deter these animals, but to date their only successful recourse has been to shoot them. For example, between 1989 and 1997 more than 3,800 harbor seals and sea lions were reported killed by salmon farmers in British Columbia alone; the actual number of creatures involved is very likely to be much higher. Although these killings do not significantly threaten future populations of these animals, the public generally disapproves when farmers resort to using guns against wildlife.

Competing with marine mammals, seabirds and farmers are the people involved in commercial salmon fisheries. Farms have produced enough to lower prices, making fishing for salmon much less profitable.

Were overfishing the only cause of the decline of wild salmon, this development might be welcomed by those interested in protecting marine life. But the fact that the numbers of wild salmon are not rebounding shows that the recent declines probably have more to do with the loss of habitat than with the problems of overfishing or aquaculture. With many rivers and streams blocked by dams, polluted by chemicals and choked by silt, salmon have found spawning runs increasingly difficult to make. People who fish for these creatures want to maintain large populations and understand that to do so freshwater habitats have to be protected. So, ironically, these fishers—

the very group most threatened by the rise of salmon aquaculture—may turn out to be among wild fish's strongest advocates.

Water in Europe's Rhine River was once in bad shape. At the turn of the twentieth century, cities dumped untreated sewage directly into the river, giving the waterway a historically wretched reputation for having a bad smell. In the 1950s, the five countries that utilize the river's resources banded together to clean it up. And it worked. Today, the Rhine River is an environmental success story and an example of what can happen when countries cooperate with one another in their reclamation efforts.

One of the largest rivers in Europe, the Rhine flows through five nations (Switzerland, France, Luxembourg, Germany, and the Netherlands) and provides drinking water for humans as well as water for industrial uses. A biological survey taken in the mid-1990s found that of the forty-seven species of fish known to have inhabited the waters, forty continue to thrive. This number includes fifteen species that had been introduced into the Rhine and a sturgeon, a species thought to be extinct in the river for decades.

*But the continued health of the river does not
happen by accident. It is maintained by a combination of careful water-quality monitors, pollution
regulations, voluntary controls, and financial
rewards to environmentally friendly farmers. This
article takes a detailed look at the Rhine River's
route, regulation, and rehabilitation. —KW*

"Cleaning Up the River Rhine"
by Karl-Geert Malle
Scientific American, January 1996

> In Köln, a town of monks and bones,
>   and pavements fanged with murderous
>   stones
> And rags, and hags, and hideous wenches;
> I counted two and seventy stenches,
> All well defined, and several stinks!
> Ye Nymphs that reign o'er sewers and
>   sinks,
> The river Rhine, it is well known,
> Doth wash your city of Cologne;
> But tell me, Nymphs, what power divine,
> Shall henceforth wash the river Rhine?

So wrote Samuel Taylor Coleridge in 1828, after a visit
to the Rhine with William Wordsworth. Just how
prophetic those lines were, Coleridge could hardly have
guessed. In the 1960s and early 1970s, as central Europe
resurged economically, organic and inorganic pollution

in the Rhine reached levels high enough to decimate or wipe out dozens of fish species and other creatures that had existed in the river for many thousands of years. Most of the river became unsuitable for swimming or bathing, and the production of drinking water was threatened.

After the 1970s, however, international attempts to clean up the Rhine, including some dating to the 1950s, finally began reclaiming long stretches of the river. Today, although much remains to be done, the work is emerging as a success story in cooperation among nations for the sake of pollution control and as a model for the many other places where transborder flows of contaminants have strained relations.

Most important, the reclamation efforts are giving new life to one of the world's great rivers. Countless poets, prose writers and lyricists have praised (or lamented) this fabled waterway, which winds through or along five countries before emptying finally through a Dutch delta into the North Sea. From Alpine headwaters in east central Switzerland, the Rhine flows 1,320 kilometers north and west through rugged mountains, lovely Lake Constance in Switzerland, the Black Forest, broad Alsatian valleys and such cities as Strasbourg, Bonn, Düsseldorf and Rotterdam. Both the Volga and the Danube are mightier and longer, but neither can match the Rhine's relatively constant flow and utility as an artery into the heart of Europe.

The catchment area, within which precipitation collects and feeds the river, covers some 190,000 square kilometers and has a population of 50 million. More than eight million of these people get their drinking water from the river, and another 10 million from Lake Constance. All told, more than 20 percent of the average flow of the Rhine is diverted and used, either for human consumption or for industrial rinsing and cooling. In addition, 10 hydroelectric plants, built after World War I and clustered in French territory below Alsace, generate a total of 8.7 million megawatt-hours every year.

The river is navigable for 800 kilometers, from the North Sea to the waterfalls below Lake Constance. Each day more than 500 barges ply its waters, laden with gasoline and other petroleum-based fuels, salt, phosphate rock, coal, gravel, new automobiles and other cargo, which adds up to about 150 million tons a year. Overall, use of the Rhine has been estimated to be five times greater than that of the Mississippi, when measured in terms of gross national product and accounting for the two rivers' flow rates and catchment populations.

One of the main reasons for the Rhine's importance is its relatively reliable water supply. In winter and spring, the flow is fed by precipitation in the plains and uplands of the catchment area; in summer, melting snow from the Alps takes over. Constance and other Swiss lakes act as convenient reservoirs. The average flow rate between 1925 and 1992 was 2,350 cubic meters per second, and the ratio between the greatest yearly flow (3,170 cubic meters per second in 1966) and the lowest (1,510 in 1971) is 2.1—less extreme than for most other rivers.

Reclamation Begins

Before the end of World War II, hardly any large sewage treatment plants were situated on the Rhine. The odors so poignantly described by Coleridge were at one time confined to the major cities, whose sewage was released untreated into the river. After the war, however, as central Europe revived its economies, the pollution problem intensified to such an extent that it could no longer be ignored. In 1953 five nations— Switzerland, France, Luxembourg, Germany and the Netherlands—formed the International Commission for the Protection of the Rhine against Pollution, to coordinate multinational effort and to monitor, at least, the levels of contaminants in the river.

The commission, known by the acronym IKSR, now monitors water quality at several fixed points, mostly at international borders. The most significant of these lies between Germany and the Netherlands, because this area is not far downstream from the heavily industrial German Ruhrgebiet. Named after the Ruhr, a small tributary of the Rhine, this region's coal, steel and chemical plants constitute one of the major sources of pollution. Moreover, after entering the Netherlands, the river passes through a fairly rural area, with no significant sources of pollution until it encounters the big Dutch harbors at Rotterdam and Amsterdam, some 150 kilometers from Germany and not far from the delta on the North Sea.

Another notable factor in this regard is the river's flow, which slows considerably in the Netherlands. After making its way from Switzerland through France and Germany within seven or eight days, the water remains for 70 or 80 days in the Netherlands because of the country's sophisticated system of dikes, canals and other water-management facilities (including two large artificial lakes, the IJsselmeer and the Haringvliet). Shortly after entering the Netherlands, the Rhine becomes a delta with three separate estuaries: the Waal, Lek and IJssel.

The IKSR issues an annual report with extensive analytical data, reviewed and confirmed by the countries within the commission. But its main business is proposing and implementing international projects to improve the river. The two most significant of these are the Convention on the Protection of the Rhine against Chemical Pollution and the Convention on the Protection of the Rhine against Chloride Pollution. Both were put into effect in 1976. Another convention, which would have addressed thermal pollution, was drafted but never ratified by all the member states. Although the river is being warmed gradually by natural trends and human activities, the degree of warming—1.8 degrees Celsius since 1925—is not considered onerous enough to merit extensive attention.

Inorganic Contaminants

Rivers typically contain far more inorganic salts than organic substances. Some of these salts are leached naturally out of the soil by rainwater and carried to the river. Through sewage, industrial activity and agriculture, however, humankind has significantly augmented the natural content. The concentration of salts—including anions such as chloride and carbonate, as well as cations such as sodium and calcium—was measured at 581 milligrams per liter at the German-Dutch border in 1992. There have been no striking changes in this level of concentration over the past two decades. Reducing the concentration of fairly dilute salts is extremely expensive, so the water is desalinated only when necessary—before being used for irrigation, for example.

Human activities have been especially productive of chloride ions. Based on the 1992 measurements, it is believed that they contribute some 318 kilograms of chloride to the river every second, as compared with the 15 to 75 kilograms per second from nature. The largest sources are the French potash mines in Alsace, which alone add 130 kilograms per second.

Sodium chloride is an unwanted byproduct of the mining, and it is either piled up on land in huge hills or dissolved and transported to the sea by the Rhine.

For decades, the practice has incensed Dutch flower growers, who depend on the water to irrigate orchids, gladioli and other flowers that react poorly to chloride. The 1976 chloride convention called for some of the salts to be stocked on land in France, with that country, Germany and the Netherlands sharing the costs. The provision was vetoed by the Alsatians, and the Dutch parliament refused to pay, so the plan never went into effect. Instead an agreement was finally reached in 1992 whereby the discharges from the mining area are controlled so that the chloride content at the German-Dutch border does not exceed 200 milligrams per liter. In practice, this means that the salts must be held back perhaps two or three times a year for a few days. Not many Dutch growers are happy with this solution, but the problem is unlikely to be resolved before the potash deposits are exhausted, sometime in the next 10 or 20 years.

Troublesome though they are, the chlorides are actually one of the lesser problems at the Dutch end of the river. Nitrogen and phosphorus, which come mostly from sewage, boost algae growth to extreme levels and artificially stimulate the food chain—a process called eutrophication. The phenomenon is of concern mainly in the slow-moving Dutch waters, where the algae can become thick enough to hinder shipping and to clog pumps. In addition, when the algae die in the autumn, their decomposition uses up the oxygen necessary to sustain fish and other creatures.

Treatment of sewage, which significantly reduces its nitrogen and phosphorus content, became more consistent in 1959, after the formation of the International Water Conservation Commission for Lake Constance. Since the early 1970s, sewage treatment plants, along with the use of phosphate-free detergents, have steadily reduced the phosphorus in the river. In 1992 an average concentration of 0.21 milligram of phosphorus per liter was measured at the German-Dutch border, which, though an improvement over previous years, is still 10 times higher than the level in Lake Constance.

Nitrogen levels, however, have not fallen significantly, and the reasons are somewhat complicated. Nitrogen in the river has two main forms: ammonium and nitrate. Over the past 20 years, treatment has reduced the ammonium to about 0.27 milligram of nitrogen per liter. Nitrate levels, on the other hand, have increased and were found in 1992 to be 3.8 milligrams of nitrogen per liter. Most of the nitrate is believed to come from fertilizers used to grow crops along the banks. Hopes that nitrate levels will not increase are pinned to various subsidy programs. For example, faced with a surplus of certain crops, the European Union gives subsidies to farmers who take land out of cultivation. Germany, meanwhile, subsidizes farmers who avoid using fertilizers in the bank zones of the river and who reduce the total use of fertilizers.

Another class of inorganic chemicals of great physiological significance are the heavy metals. In trace concentrations, some of these metals are essential to life. In higher concentrations, they can cause nervous system, growth and metabolic disorders. Mercury, cadmium, copper and some chromium come mainly from metal and chemical plants, which are easily identified and therefore controlled. Nickel, zinc and the rest of the chromium get into the river with the sewage effluent as a result of corrosion of pipes and equipment in homes and industrial plants and so are harder to restrict. Lead has been minimized through its removal from gasoline. The river's minute traces of gold do not endanger human health. (In the early 19th century untold numbers of prospectors panned for the metal along the banks of the upper Rhine, between the Swiss border and Worms in Germany.) Overall, the amount of these metals in the Rhine has declined by more than 90 percent since the early 1970s. Sewage treatment plants have also helped by immobilizing large amounts in the sludge. In addition, programs have been instituted at industrial dischargers, by which the metals are selectively retained for reuse.

For the most part, the metal content in the Rhine's waters is no longer sufficient to harm people or marine life. But the sediments underneath certain parts of the riverbed and its tributaries are still quite metallic. Problems persist at the heavily industrial port of Rotterdam as well. Excavation there has dredged up metal-laden sediments, which have remained suspended in nearby estuaries. Protracted negotiations between the port authorities and some upstream metal and chemical industries have led to private-law contracts intended to reduce further the amount of metals that are released.

Organic Ogres

Whereas the monitoring and control of inorganic substances are useful in any river, water quality overall is generally much more sensitive to organic pollutants. Although such organics are usually no more than 1 percent of the pollution in a river, they tend to use up its dissolved oxygen, making the water unfit for sustaining life.

Between 1969 and 1976, organic pollution peaked in the Rhine, frequently sending dissolved oxygen levels below two milligrams per liter in some parts of the middle and lower river during the summer months. Such levels are not high enough to sustain many organisms. Since then, Germany alone has spent some $55 billion on sewage treatment plants, which retain about 90 percent of the organic pollutants. Dissolved oxygen has returned to healthier levels of about nine or 10 milligrams per liter (about 90 percent of the amount the water can physically contain in solution).

In comparison with the monitoring of inorganic pollutants, keeping tabs on organic substances is considerably more complex. Although inorganic chemicals may account for 99 percent of the pollution in a river, their number generally adds up to only several dozen. In contrast, organic constituents, of both natural and artificial origin, are more likely to number in the thousands. Isolating and analyzing each of them is not feasible, so researchers usually group them into various categories and employ different methods to track them. One commonly used technique establishes the effects or characteristics of all organic substances in the water. Another determines the concentrations of groups of similar compounds. Together these techniques can give a useful estimate of the organic state of a body of water and can be supplemented by measurements of single organic substances as needed.

One of the most common measurements in the first category is the biological oxygen demand, typically within a five-day period (abbreviated BOD_5). Bacteria and nutrients are added to the water, and their consumption of oxygen is recorded, generally in milligrams per liter of water. Another good measurement is known as chemical oxygen demand (COD), in which concentrated sulfuric acid and chromium are used to establish the maximum possible oxygen consumption of the sample. In 1992 at the German-Dutch border, the BOD_5 was measured at an average of three milligrams per liter; the COD was 10 milligrams per liter.

Substances commonly grouped together fall into four broad categories: adsorbable organic halogens (AOX, which refers primarily to compounds that contain chlorine); detergents; hydrocarbons; and humic acids. Even as part of larger molecules, chlorine and other halogens are especially worrisome because of their toxicity and persistence. Chlorine compounds

Levels of Dissolved Oxygen in the Rhine

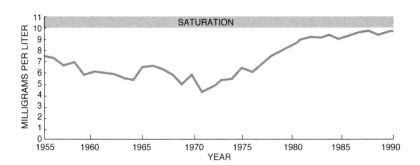

Life-sustaining oxygen levels reached a nadir around the summer of 1970, when amounts in certain parts of the Rhine were too low to keep many creatures alive.

Organic Pollutants in the Rhine

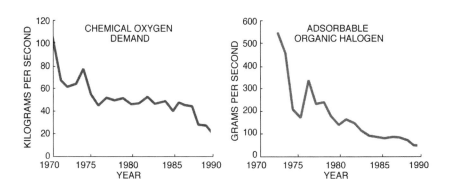

Oxygen consumption by organic pollutants, as well as the influx of such compounds containing halogens (mainly chlorine), has fallen dramatically since 1970.

come from several sources, including cellulose factories, which bleach raw cellulose to whiten it for making paper. Most of these factories have been converted to low- or even no-chlorine bleaching processes. Chlorine has also entered the river in the form of insecticides, such as DDT (dichlorodiphenyltrichloroethane), HCH (hexachlorocyclohexane), HCB (hexachlorobenzene) and PCP (pentachlorophenol). Germany no longer produces or permits the use of these chemicals. DDT and HCB are similarly banned by other countries along the Rhine, and the use of HCH, PCP and other persistent chlorinated compounds is tightly restricted by these and other countries. Since the mid-1970s, such measures have helped reduce the levels of some organic chlorine compounds at the German-Dutch border by factors between 5 and 15.

Substitution of less persistent pollutants has also been effective in controlling surfactants, the active ingredients of detergents. Since 1964, Germany has permitted only detergents that are readily biodegradable. This restriction has been key in reducing anionic surfactants (the most common kind), as measured in the waters flowing by Düsseldorf, from 650 grams per second in 1964 to 80 grams per second in 1987. In 1992 all measurements for anionic surfactants at the German-Dutch border were below 0.05 milligram per liter.

Hydrocarbons are more readily biodegradable than the halogenated compounds. Petroleum products such as gasoline, kerosene and naphtha account for about 20 percent of all upstream traffic carried on the Rhine across the Dutch border. In addition, the bilges of the thousands of vessels that use the Rhine every year collect some 20,000 cubic meters of an oil-and-water admixture, most of which is collected and removed by special-purpose boats. Such measures are keeping hydrocarbon concentrations down to 0.01 milligram per liter at the Dutch border.

The fourth grouping of organic substances—the humic acids—are the short-term products of biodegradation, one of the most potent tools of reclaimers. Yet whether it is induced in a sewage treatment plant or takes place naturally in the river itself, biodegradation is a never-ending process. Only part of the organic substances consumed by bacteria is fully metabolized and respirated as carbon dioxide. The rest are only partly oxidized and thereby converted into humic acids. Although produced in sewage treatment plants, they have always been in the river. In 1973 humic acids were estimated to account for about 25 percent of the residual organic pollution of the Rhine. More recently, this fraction has increased, although the percentage is difficult to determine because of the lack of analytical methods. Humic acids are considered essentially harmless, however, because they are produced early on in the natural, gradual oxidation of organic material in any river.

A Seminal Accident

No matter how carefully certain pollutants are controlled, the Rhine, like any heavily trafficked waterway, remains vulnerable to the occasional accident. At one time, accidents went mostly unnoticed amid the high background level of pollution. Today's cleaner river, however, reacts more profoundly to such events, and a sensitive early-warning system has been put in place to alert authorities when accidents occur.

A few unfortunate episodes were pivotal in getting the monitoring system up and running. In one of the worst, on November 1, 1986, a Sandoz Ltd. warehouse full of pesticides caught fire near Basel. Water sprayed on the fire washed the chemicals into the river, where one of them—disulfoton—proved especially toxic to eels. Many thousands were killed downstream, all the way to Karlsruhe.

The disaster triggered an effort of unprecedented scope to follow the Rhine's recovery and to assess the biological state of the river in general. During the project, biologists from a German government research institute used a diving bell to study fish, macroinvertebrates and other creatures systematically in the riverbed. To the surprise of many, the river's fauna completely recovered by October 1988, less than two years after the fire.

The survey documented 155 species of macroinvertebrates, which tend to cluster near the banks, between Basel and Düsseldorf. Some of the most common were freshwater sponges, leeches, zebra mussels, benthic amphipods, mayflies, caddis flies and worms, and chironomid larvae. Some species, such as the mayfly *Ephoron virgo* and the snail *Theodosus fluviatilis*, had been thought to be virtually extinct in the Rhine but were found in large quantities. Other once common species, such as the mussel *Spaericum solidum* or the stonefly *Euleuctea geniculata*, were present as individual specimens and are only now starting to reestablish themselves in greater numbers. Somewhat disconcertingly, however, an amphipod, *Corophium curvispinum*, a relatively recent arrival from the Caspian and Black seas, is proliferating extensively enough to drive out certain species of sponges and mollusks.

Some fish, too, are making a comeback. Of the 47 endemic species known to have inhabited the river, a recent survey found 40. About 75 percent of the individual fish identified were hardy, unspecialized creatures, including roach, bleak and bream. Researchers also spotted carp, perch, eel, pike, chub and dace. In addition, they tallied 15 species that had been introduced into the river, including pike-perch, rainbow trout and sunfish. In 1992, for the first time in decades, sexually mature salmon (*Salmo salar*) were caught in the Rhine. Released as hatchlings into tributaries of the river a year or more previously, they had survived a migration to the North Sea. Even sturgeon—believed extinct from the river for 40 years—have been seen occasionally.

A Model River

The river survey was not the only legacy of the 1986 warehouse fire in Basel. The states bordering the Rhine launched a joint Rhine Action Program, with four objectives: long-term safeguarding of the drinking water; decontamination of sediments; reestablishment of higher species of fish (salmon and so on); and protection of the North Sea.

As a first step, in 1989 the program compiled an inventory of all discharges of 30 different hazardous substances. By 1995 the rates of discharge for all had been reduced by 50 percent or more. In addition, improved safeguards prevent or limit discharges into the river after industrial accidents. In coming years, the construction of fish ladders to help creatures such as salmon get back to their upstream spawning grounds and the improvement of those grounds will begin to restore runs.

In 1991, at a conference on the waterworks in the Rhine's catchment area, the Dutch minister for transport and public works, Hanja Maij-Weggen, called for the experience acquired on the Rhine to be applied to the Meuse and Scheldt rivers. With the end of the cold war, international commissions have been set up to reclaim the Elbe, which flows from the Czech Republic and Poland through Germany to the North Sea, and the Oder, which forms part of the border between Poland and Germany. Even the Volga has benefited from lessons learned on the Rhine, which were passed on from German experts to their Russian counterparts in a recent series of meetings. For the Danube, reclamation will have to wait: work on the river has been suspended because of the war in the former Yugoslavia.

Amid sweeping changes in Europe it is fitting that the Rhine has become a tribute to the great things that can happen when countries cooperate.

The Author

Karl-Geert Malle recently retired from BASF in Ludwigshafen, Germany. After joining that company in 1960, he worked in inorganic research and in various production units before taking on the responsibility of monitoring all wastewater discharges. In 1984 he headed special tasks in environmental protection and was appointed a director. He is a member of a working committee of the German Commission for the Protection of the Rhine and of the Commission for the Evaluation of Water-Endangering Substances. He lectures on ecological chemistry at the Technical College in Mannheim.

3 | Land

The land is often used as a place to store garbage. In its simplest form, when garbage is stored, it is layered with dirt in holes in the ground called landfills. Here, the waste is shielded on the bottom with plastic liners and covered on the top with soil, both to prevent or slow pollution escaping into the environment. Waste from many different sources ends up in landfills—including waste from chicken farms.

The United States' poultry industry is the largest producer and exporter of poultry products in the world. Each year, this hugely successful industry generates 4 billion pounds (almost 2 billion kilograms) of unwanted feathers. What can one do with all those feathers? Most end up in landfills.

To keep our landfills from filling up with feathers, scientists are exploring other disposal options. One of the latest is recycling feathers for use in plastic and paper products. The following article explains a new method to break down chicken feathers into usable parts, which can be sold and used to make new plastics. If all the *feathers in the United States were recycled in this way, says the author, there would be plenty of plastic to go around. Five billion pounds (2.3 billion kilograms) of plastic, to be exact. —KW*

"Car Parts from Chickens"
by Diane Martindale
Scientific American, April 2000

Nearly a decade ago poultry-processing plants around the nation asked researchers at the Department of Agriculture to solve a big environmental problem: find a more efficient way to dispose of the four billion pounds of chicken feathers produced annually in the U.S. What they were expecting was a method by which the feathers could be made more biodegradable after burial. But Walter Schmidt, a chemist at the Agricultural Research Service (ARS) in Beltsville, Md., went a step further to develop a recycling technology that will soon bring feathers into everyday life disguised as plastic and paper products.

Currently poultry farmers mix water with leftover feathers in large pressure cookers to make low-grade feedstuff for chickens and cattle—a venture that is generally not profitable. But converting feathers into value-added products required more than just a little steam. Schmidt and his colleagues developed an efficient mechanical method to separate the more valuable barb fibers (plumage) from the less useful central chaff, or quill. Though softer, the keratin fibers in the barbs are stronger and less brittle than those in the quill and therefore have a much broader range of applications.

The key to easy separation lay in the fact that the quills are bulkier and heavier. The feathers, dried and sterilized, are shredded and fed into a cylindrical device consisting of an outer and inner tube. The feathers are sucked through the central channel, and the quills are drawn off at the bottom, but thanks to air turbulence, the barbs float back up between the sides of the tubes.

Once separated, barb fibers can be used in many ways. Schmidt and his collaborators have made diaper filler, paper towels and water filters out of them. The ground fibers have been used in plastics, in pulp to make paper, and in combination with synthetic and natural fibers to make textiles. And the fibers are good for more chemically complex applications as well. For instance, by mixing the fiber powder with a reducing agent and placing the slurry in a hydraulic press, Attila Pavlath, a scientist for the ARS in California, has created polymer films. "The reducing agent acts like a hairdresser's perm solution to relax the protein bonds of the keratin, allowing us to mold the fiber into thin sheets of plastic," Pavlath explains. This polymer may first show up as biodegradable candy wrappers (similar to cellophane) and six-pack can-holders.

The powder can also replace additives, such as nonrecyclable fiberglass, that are used to strengthen plastic. Combined with polyethylene, the barbs can produce a more rigid plastic suitable for dog-food bowls and automobile interior parts, including the dashboard.

The quill portion doesn't have to go to waste, either. David Emery of Featherfiber Corporation in Nixa, Mo., has developed a process to make high-grade quill protein that is 90 percent digestible (typical quill meal is only 50 percent digestible), Emery says. The company has licensed Schmidt's patents and has just completed a pilot plant to produce feather fiber.

Farm animals may not be the only ones to benefit from a quill meal. Carlo Licata of MaXim LLC in Pasadena, Calif., believes that the quill portion is an excellent dietary supplement for humans. "That's because the keratin protein is very absorbent," Licata indicates, "and can retain nutrients for a longer period"—something like Metamucil, only better.

All this and more from chicken feathers without breaking the farm. "A typical farm produces 10,000 pounds of feathers per hour, which is enough to meet the needs of one plastic-producing plant," Schmidt remarks. If all the feathers in the U.S. were processed, more than five billion pounds of plastic products could be made.

Feather-derived plastics are just one of several nonpetroleum-based "green plastics" that have surfaced in the past year. Cargill-Dow Polymers in Minnetonka, Minn., recently announced production of a new kind of natural plastic made from polylactic acid, a compound derived from corn. Monsanto, maker of genetically modified plants, reported last October that it had fabricated a plant capable of producing biodegradable plastic of a type known as polyhydroxyalkanoate.

But the consequences of producing greener plastics are often overlooked, according to Tillman Gerngross, a biochemical engineer at Dartmouth College. "People too readily accept the premise that renewable equals environmentally good. It does not necessarily add up." If you have to use huge amounts of coal to make the plastics, then you are harming the environment just the same, he points out. And feather plastics are often only partially biodegradable. Still, Gerngross agrees that a move toward sustainable resources is desirable. That should prevent researchers like Walter Schmidt from chickening out too soon.

The land has always been the easiest place to store nonbiodegradable waste. Nonbiodegradable waste is something that cannot be decomposed by biological agents such as bacteria. Because it does not decompose and is often piled in landfills as garbage, nonbiodegradable waste can build up in the earth and become a serious source of pollution.

In an ideal world, all the nonbiodegradable products we use would be replaced with bio-degradable ones. But we do not live in an ideal world. Even when a biodegradable replacement exists, it is often not as cheap or efficient to produce as some nonbiodegradable products. And it is almost always harder to find. This combination of factors makes the replacement more expensive and more difficult for industry to use, so industry often doesn't make the substitute available.

The following article is about an organic chemist's efforts to replace one nonbiodegradable ingredient with a biodegradable one. When he realized that a nonbiodegradable ingredient commonly used in disposable diapers and laundry detergents could be replaced with a biodegradable one, he started his own company to manufacture the substitute. But it wasn't that easy. Only when he and his employees were able to produce the new ingredient at a cheap price did their business begin to take off. They are still working on it, and they're developing new products as well. —KW

"It's Not Easy Being Green"
by Steven Ashley
Scientific American, April 2002

Larry Koskan's moment of inspiration arrived in the mid-1980s, when the organic chemist read a report by marine biologists at Clemson University and the University of South Alabama describing how oyster shells grow. Scientists knew that the mollusks secrete calcium carbonate as the essential constituent of their hardened exteriors. But what was new was the discovery that oysters also produce special protein-based agents that mold the mineral into their shells' characteristic shape. "When I realized that very low doses of the biopolymer they'd found—polyaspartate— inhibit the formation of calcium carbonate, the hair on the back of my neck rose up," Koskan recalls.

At the time, Koskan was employed by Nalco Chemical Company, where he was studying the properties of water-soluble polyacrylates (polyacrylics). Among other things, these widely used polymer additives help to stem the buildup of damaging mineral scale deposits (carbonate and sulfate compounds) on the surfaces of industrial water-treatment equipment. He realized that biodegradable polyaspartate could do the same job.

Polyaspartate mimics the scale-inhibiting activity of polyacrylate because it has a similar chemical morphology. Both molecules feature an active carboxylate chemical group directly attached to the polymer building blocks—a configuration that accounts for their chemical function, Koskan explains. But because the polymer backbone of polyaspartate is made of peptides (chains of amino acids) rather than the hydrocarbon compounds that constitute polyacrylate's backbone, it is degradable by bacterial action.

Polyacrylates, inexpensive and versatile chemicals that are easy to manufacture and process, have one drawback: they last virtually forever. "For years, the first question I'd hear when making customer calls in Germany and elsewhere in Europe was, 'Are your acrylic polymers biodegradable?'" Koskan says, noting that European governments were encouraging industry there to use environmentally friendly products. He suspected that he'd spotted an answer to their prayers as well as a potential winner in the then emerging "green chemistry" market.

The chemist's interest in the new polyaspartates was further piqued by the possibility that the biodegradable compounds could substitute for polyacrylics in other commercial roles. "In detergents, for example, water-soluble acrylates act as dispersants that keep dirt suspended in the wash water," Koskan says. Nowadays some half a billion pounds of polyacrylates are used in laundry detergents worldwide every year.

Even more enticing was the chance to enter another fast-growing market for polyacrylics: superabsorbent materials for disposable baby diapers and feminine-hygiene and adult-incontinence products, which currently account for around two billion pounds in annual production of polyacrylates. The polyacrylic chains crosslink into weblike configurations with a tremendous affinity for water. The trouble is, vast quantities of the highly stable substance are discarded in landfills.

When Koskan realized in ensuing years that Nalco Chemical had little interest in expending the considerable time and money it would take to pursue the polyaspartate technology, he decided to form his own company. Working with Ernst & Young, the accounting services firm, he developed a financial package for the start-up venture. In 1990 Donlar Corporation—now called Donlar Biosyntrex, after a recent merger—opened its doors in Bedford, Ill. (Today it has 17 employees.)

Around the same time, consumer products giant Procter & Gamble was removing phosphate watersoftening additives from its popular laundry detergents. Such agents are environmentally undesirable because they can lead to the eutrophication (overenrichment) of surface waters, causing algae blooms.

"P&G started using significant quantities of polyacrylates as dispersants in its new detergents, as well as in disposable diapers and other superabsorbent products," notes Bob Pietrangelo, a veteran chemical industry executive who is now Donlar's chief operating officer. With the use of polyacrylates rising, P&G prodded the chemical industry to develop biodegradable substitutes for them. Soon thereafter, leading companies, including Rohm and Haas, BASF and Bayer, were researching the issue. "After six or seven years," Pietrangelo continues, "virtually everybody settled on polyaspartate as the most suitable replacement."

Unfortunately, the price of the substitute was estimated to be four to five times that of the high-volume-production polyacrylates. "The problem for emerging technologies such as polyaspartates in securing a market niche is that the supporting infrastructure—particularly sufficient capacity to manufacture the product at a competitive price—is not generally available," Pietrangelo says. "As polyaspartates would be a costly product in small quantities, P&G lost interest and walked away from the technology, so the industry didn't run with it." Donlar, however, decided to stick with its core business and to focus on specialty application niches. "We spent the next five years after we set up Donlar developing the chemistry and the process technology for polyaspartates so we could offer competitive market pricing," Koskan recounts. So far the company has invested more than $50 million on development.

Donlar's patented production process starts with L‑aspartic acid, a natural amino acid. It is heated on trays, causing the amino acid to polymerize as the constituent water is driven out. This reaction results in an intermediate powder product called polysuccinimide, a ring-shaped molecular compound. No solvents are required, and the only by-product is steam, which can be reused in the process. In the second step the polysuccinimide is hydrolyzed to polyaspartate through the addition of water, heat and a caustic base such as sodium hydroxide. Raising the pH of the mixture opens up the molecular rings, which form long polymer chains of sodium polyaspartate (a salt of alpha-beta-DL-polyaspartic acid). Donlar markets the result as thermal polyaspartate, or TPA. In 1997 the company completed a 50,000-square-foot manufacturing plant in Peru, Ill., with a production capacity of more than 30 million pounds a year.

Despite Donlar's success in developing the technology (and despite winning the first Green Chemistry Challenge Award from the U.S. Environmental Protection Agency in 1996), sales of the biodegradable product were not a sure bet. Says Pietrangelo: "It's a funny thing about being environmentally friendly: everybody's in favor of it, but nobody wants to pay more for it." Koskan agrees: "Though TPA is a tremendous technology, we had to forget about its green chemistry aspects and go with the idea that we've got a novel product that is competitive based on its merits."

By offering various technical advantages in certain applications, TPA has garnered increased sales in the oil and agricultural markets in recent years. (The company as a whole did $6.4 million in sales in 2000.) British Petroleum Exploration and other energy companies working the difficult North Sea offshore oil fields have achieved success with a TPA additive that helps to sustain the flow of crude from oil wells. In these operations, production is facilitated by injecting seawater under the ocean floor to maintain the pressure in the underlying oil formations. Because of the incompatibility of seawater with the water in the undersea geologic formation, mineral scales would otherwise form and block the flow of oil. Dual-purpose TPA not only inhibits mineral scale formation but checks oxidation as well.

In farming applications, the same TPA formulation is being added to fertilizers to keep them in the soil longer, allowing plant roots to absorb more nutrients.

The result is greater crop yields and reduced nitrate runoff into groundwater. Donlar researchers have developed other products as well. For example, they have succeeded in cross-linking polyaspartate chains to produce a biodegradable superabsorbent material that could find widespread use at some point.

If Donlar can show continued success, it may help revive an environmental chemistry sector saddled with a reputation for ineffectiveness and high cost. And, as a profitable venture, it may finally lend an additional meaning to the "green" in green chemistry.

Steven Ashley is a staff editor and writer.

The land may someday be used to store radio-active garbage produced by nuclear power plants and military operations. The trick is finding a place in the earth that everyone agrees is safe. To be safe, the location can't be near earthquake regions (called fault zones) or be wet. Water could destroy canisters protecting radioactive waste and become contaminated.

In the United States, a ridgeline 99 miles (160 kilometers) northwest of Las Vegas, Nevada, called Yucca Mountain has been studied for nearly twenty years to determine if it is a safe place to store the nation's radioactive *garbage. So far, the federal government has spent about $8 billion (and counting) on scientific and technical studies as well as other expenses. In addition, the state of Nevada has hired its own scientists to study the site and strongly opposes building a facility in the mountain.*

This article explains the issues being studied at Yucca Mountain and how people could be exposed to radiation if something goes wrong. In the end, author Chris G. Whipple suggests it is impossible to predict exactly what could happen to the mountain in the future or if it will ever be approved as a place to store the nation's radioactive garbage. —KW

"Can Nuclear Waste Be Stored Safely at Yucca Mountain?"
by Chris G. Whipple
Scientific American, June 1996

In the half century of the nuclear age, the U.S. has accumulated some 30,000 metric tons of spent fuel rods from power reactors and another 380,000 cubic meters of high-level radioactive waste, a by-product of producing plutonium for nuclear weapons. None of these materials have found anything more than interim accommodation, despite decades of study and expenditures in the billions of dollars on research, development and storage.

The fuel rods, which accumulate at the rate of six tons a day, have for the most part remained at the nuclear reactors where they were irradiated, in water-filled basins and, in some cases, in steel containers on concrete pads. The high-level waste occupies huge, aging tanks at government sites in Washington State, South Carolina, Idaho and New York State. Some tanks have leaked, making conspicuous the lack of a more permanent, efficient and coherent solution for the nuclear waste problem.

In 1987 the federal government narrowed to one its long-term options for disposing of this waste: storing it permanently in a series of caverns excavated out of the rock deep below Yucca Mountain in southern Nevada. Since then, the U.S. Department of Energy, which is responsible for the handling of practically all the high-level nuclear waste in the U.S., has spent $1.7 billion on scientific and technical studies of whether such a repository below the mountain might safely store waste.

From the very beginning, however, the state of Nevada has strongly opposed the project, hiring its own scientists to study the mountain. Whether the state can block the project altogether is uncertain; its active opposition, though, is sure to complicate an undertaking that is already very difficult.

At the same time, legal issues make it necessary that something be done. Since 1982, nuclear utilities in the U.S. have paid $12 billion into a Nuclear Waste Fund and a related escrow account. In return, the DOE pledged to build a national repository and begin accepting the utilities' waste in 1998. Yet even if a repository is actually built at Yucca Mountain, it could not begin accepting waste until after 2015, according to the latest estimates. This has prompted the utilities to file suit in the U.S. Court of Appeals in Washington, D.C., to find out exactly what they are owed in two years' time. In addition, legal agreements with the states of Washington and South Carolina oblige the DOE to process the high-level tank waste into glass logs, for eventual disposal in a repository.

Whether it makes sense at this time to dispose permanently of spent fuel and radioactive waste in a deep geologic repository is hotly disputed. But the Nuclear Waste Policy Act amendments of 1987 decree that waste be consolidated in Yucca Mountain if the mountain is found suitable. Meanwhile the spent fuel continues to pile up across the country, and 1998 looms, adding urgency to the question: What can science tell us about the ability of Yucca Mountain to store nuclear waste safely?

Tuff Enough?

The answer, or at least part of it, is to be found deep under that barren mound of rock, where preliminary work has already begun on an exploratory tunnel. Yucca Mountain, about 160 kilometers northwest of Las Vegas, is adjacent to the Nevada Test Site, where until recently, the DOE tested nuclear weapons. The mountain might more accurately be described as a ridge, about 29 kilometers long and jutting up several hundred meters above the surrounding land. It is composed of tuff, a rock formed from volcanic ash, estimated to be between 11 million and 13 million years old.

Although many design details have not yet been made final, the plan is for canisters containing spent fuel to be arranged horizontally in chambers 300 meters below the surface and 240 to 370 meters above the water table. Once the repository was full, it would be monitored for at least 50 years and then sealed.

Although alternatives, such as disposing of radioactive waste beneath the ocean floor or even in outer space, have been considered, the U.S. and all other countries with high-level waste disposal programs have chosen to pursue deep geologic repositories, such as the one planned for Yucca Mountain. Still, no country has yet disposed of any spent fuel or high-level waste in such a repository. At this time, the only real alternative to a repository is long-term storage above ground; while less expensive, such storage is not a means of disposal, because the materials still have to be maintained and continuously secured. A hybrid proposal—to store spent fuel and high-level waste in a subterranean repository but to keep the facility open indefinitely—has also been suggested.

The Yucca Mountain repository would be accessed through a pair of tunnels comprising the sides of a U-shaped loop through the mountain, with the repository at the trough [see illustration on pages 142 and 143]. The gently sloping tunnels are an attractive feature made possible by the site's mountainous topography. Half of the U-shaped loop has been excavated, providing

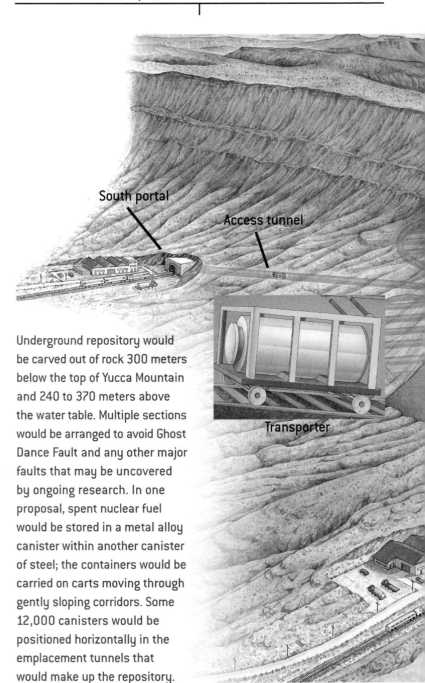

South portal

Access tunnel

Transporter

Underground repository would be carved out of rock 300 meters below the top of Yucca Mountain and 240 to 370 meters above the water table. Multiple sections would be arranged to avoid Ghost Dance Fault and any other major faults that may be uncovered by ongoing research. In one proposal, spent nuclear fuel would be stored in a metal alloy canister within another canister of steel; the containers would be carried on carts moving through gently sloping corridors. Some 12,000 canisters would be positioned horizontally in the emplacement tunnels that would make up the repository.

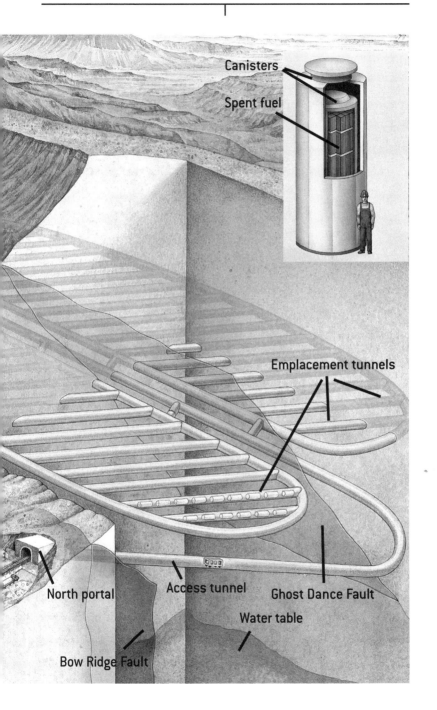

Canisters

Spent fuel

Emplacement tunnels

North portal

Access tunnel

Ghost Dance Fault

Water table

Bow Ridge Fault

access for studies of the mountain's interior. The sloping tunnel has penetrated about five kilometers into the mountain and has reached the location of the proposed repository. Rapid progress is now being made with a 7.6- meter-diameter tunnel-boring machine, which excavates up to 30 meters of rock a day.

Designers anticipate dividing the repository into two sections laid out to avoid major geologic faults. Finding and characterizing those faults is the goal of several projects that are about to begin. The poetically named Ghost Dance Fault, the largest and most important, divides the region of the repository in two. In fact, a more detailed repository design mainly awaits more information on Ghost Dance and the other faults that run through the general volume where the chambers will be excavated.

Current plans call for a repository large enough to hold 70,000 metric tons of spent nuclear fuel. Of this tonnage, 90 percent (63,000 tons) would be spent fuel from commercial power plants, and the remaining 10 percent (7,000 tons) would be defense wastes. For these wastes, the 7,000-ton limit refers to the spent fuel that was originally irradiated, thus creating the waste, which is now actually a mix of liquids and solids.

The 63,000-ton target would cover most, but not all, of the commercial spent fuel generated in the U.S., if no new reactors are built and if those now operating have lives of 40 years. The estimate is that the inventory of fuel from U.S. power reactors will amount to around 84,000 tons by the time they have reached the limit of their licensed operating life. Yet the 7,000-ton allocation for defense wastes would not even contain the DOE's inventory of wastes and spent fuel from Hanford alone. Currently no policy exists to designate a site for a second repository.

Besides the activities aimed at revealing the geologic features and properties of Yucca Mountain, DOE scientists are evaluating how alternative repository designs would affect long-term performance and how various waste-package designs and materials would contribute to the repository's ability to isolate hazardous wastes from the environment.

How People Might Be Exposed

A great deal of effort has gone into discovering and analyzing the ways in which humans could be exposed to radioactive materials from a waste repository. Dozens of scenarios have been offered. In the one that has received the most attention, waste canisters corrode, and water leaches radioactive elements (radionuclides) out of the spent fuel or vitrified high-level waste, then carries them into the groundwater. People would be exposed if they used the water for any of the usual purposes: drinking, washing or irrigation.

A repository at Yucca Mountain, however, would have some inherent resistance to such occurrences. The repository would store the waste above the groundwater, in what is known as unsaturated rock. Depending on how much water flows down through the mountain and contacts the waste, the movement of radioactive materials into groundwater can be delayed for a long time and can occur at a limited rate in comparison to what might occur at a site below the water table.

An additional advantage is that repository operations, including the possibility of retrieval of the spent fuel or repair of the repository if needed, would be simpler in unsaturated rock. Whereas the prospects for intentional retrieval of spent fuel are seen by some as remote or threatening to nonproliferation, to others the discarding of spent fuel is extremely profligate. Given the enormous energy content of the plutonium and uranium in the spent fuel, intentional retrieval of these materials at some distant time is a reasonable possibility that must be recognized. Retrieval of spent fuel would be easier from Yucca Mountain than from some of the other types of repositories that have been considered.

The probability that people will some day come into contact with radionuclides from Yucca Mountain, and the magnitude of the dose they might receive, depends on many factors. Some factors can be fairly well quantified for any future time; others cannot. In the former category is the content of the waste, determined by taking into account the radioactive decay of some isotopes and the consequent growth of others. Similarly, the dilution and dispersion of the radionuclides in groundwater as the water seeps away from the repository is believed to be calculable with reasonable accuracy, based on well-understood mechanisms and knowledge of many existing contamination plumes.

On the other hand, a significant unknown at this time is the infiltration rate—the rate at which water percolates down through the mountain. Only about 16 centimeters of rain falls on Yucca Mountain every year. Most of this water evaporates, although some does penetrate the ground. Its movement is the single most important factor in determining how long the buried canisters might survive—their rate of corrosion depends strongly on how much moisture they encounter. Flow rates are estimated from the age of water found in the zone above the water table; the age of the water is calculated from carbon, chlorine and uranium isotope ratios.

Still, the variability in the rainwater infiltration rate throughout the mountain may prove difficult to characterize, and the possibility that climate changes will produce a higher flux cannot be dismissed. On the other hand, layers of caliche, a form of calcium carbonate, or other comparatively impermeable materials could serve as barriers to restrict the downward migration of water.

Projections of how radionuclides might move from the repository into groundwater are also complex and uncertain. If water flows primarily through fractures in the rock, the transportation time would be relatively short, with little retardation of radionuclides by zeolites—silicate-based rock that tends to retain many chemicals. But if the downward flow is largely through the rock itself, the travel time and retardation of radionuclides would be greater. The actual mix of fracture flow and through-rock seepage cannot be known precisely, because the entire mountain cannot be analyzed in the fine detail needed.

Human settlement patterns present an even greater challenge. One of the most significant uncertainties in risk calculations for a planned repository such as at Yucca Mountain comes from the need to make assumptions about where people will live and work. What will occur in far-future times is of course unknowable, but assumptions can be made for purposes of hypothetical projections. Basically, for a Yucca Mountain repository to pose a hazard, people must live over or near a plume of groundwater contaminated by leakage from the repository, use water wells sunk into the plume and fail to detect that the water has been contaminated.

Other release scenarios have also been considered. They include events that might result from volcanism near Yucca Mountain and from inadvertent human intrusion in connection with, for example, mining. The U.S. Geological Survey and other DOE contractors have been studying volcanoes in the vicinity to try to estimate the likelihood of future activity, which appears improbable. Earthquakes are also being studied, but the historical evidence indicates that earthquakes tend to be much less harmful to underground structures than to surface ones. The speculation about whether and how inadvertent human intrusion might occur is much like attempts to determine the type of society that might occupy Yucca Mountain: interesting to think about but unknowable.

How Safe Is "Safe"?

Difficulties in making realistic projections are exacerbated by uncertainties about standards. The question of whether nuclear waste can be stored safely at Yucca Mountain naturally prompts another query: What exactly is meant by "safe?" That question cannot yet be answered; from a regulatory viewpoint, the DOE is working toward an as yet undefined standard. In 1992 Congress directed the Environmental Protection Agency and the National Research Council (NRC) to develop new standards, specific to Yucca Mountain, based on recommendations from the National Academy of Sciences. The academy's guidelines have been published, and the EPA's new standards are still being developed. The NRC is expected to put forth its proposals after the EPA does.

One of the most fundamental unresolved questions concerns the length of time that the repository would be required to contain the waste. Until recently, the timescale under consideration was the EPA's limit of 10,000 years. But for Yucca Mountain, that limit has been challenged by the National Academy of Sciences's recent recommendations to the EPA and NRC. The academy's view is that the repository should contain the waste until its risk begins to decline—even if that means a million years. How the EPA and NRC will respond to this recommendation is not yet known.

It appears quite plausible that if the canisters and other packaging were appropriately designed, a Yucca

Mountain repository could prevent waste from migrating in significant quantities into the environment for 10,000 years. The projected life of a waste package is based on corrosion rates for different package materials and repository conditions. For Yucca Mountain, experts are considering various alloys of steel and titanium, as well as ceramic materials.

It is in waste-package life that, unfortunately, some of the advantages of an unsaturated repository are offset. Specifically, the chemical conditions in an unsaturated repository favor oxidation—that is, they tend to promote reaction with oxygen. A well-chosen saturated site, in contrast, could be a reducing environment; it would tend to prevent reactions between metals and oxygen.

The challenges of developing long-lived waste packages in an oxidizing environment appear to be more difficult than for a reducing environment. For example, the Swedish program for spent-fuel disposal plans to use copper-coated canisters in a saturated repository near a seacoast. The Swedes estimate that a million-year canister life can be anticipated. An added "benefit" of the Swedish approach is that if the repository does eventually begin to leak, it will do so into the ocean, not into a potable aquifer.

For an unsaturated, oxidizing environment, ceramics may be the best choice for packaging waste because they have the advantage of already being oxidized. Cathodic protection of multiple-layer canisters, in which an outer layer electrically shields an inner layer, also appears to extend waste-package life significantly.

Research into the deterioration of waste packages has found that corrosion occurs most rapidly to canisters in contact with liquid water, such as a recurrent drip onto the waste package or the accumulation of a puddle under a package. If the repository design can eliminate direct water contact, the next most important factor is humidity. Tests indicate that the corrosion rate for candidate materials is very low—almost zero—below a threshold humidity but that corrosion progresses faster at higher humidities. Unfortunately, the ambient humidity inside Yucca Mountain is high, around 98 to 99 percent, and therefore corrosive for most candidate waste-package materials.

The observation that liquid water and high humidity accelerate waste-package failure has led to what is known as the hot, dry repository concept. Raising the temperature of the surrounding rock to above the boiling point of water, using heat from the waste itself, would effectively eliminate levels of humidity or accumulations of liquid water that could cause corrosion of waste packages. Calculations indicate that for comparatively high waste-packing densities, above 200 tons of uranium per hectare, for example, the repository temperature could be kept above boiling for more than 10,000 years.

The downside is that such elevated temperatures may also adversely affect materials in the repository and the mountain—for example, more heat may increase the rate of canister degradation. The DOE is currently considering this trade-off and has not yet determined what operating temperature it would seek to maintain in the repository.

Over a timescale of hundreds of thousands of years, all safety analyses presume that canisters have failed and that the rock between the repository and the groundwater has achieved equilibrium with the waste products migrating through. In this case, the capability of the rock to retard the movement of waste has been fully taxed. Radionuclide concentrations in water flowing down from the repository and the radiation exposures resulting from use of this water are both in a steady state. The key factors in this process are the water's rate of flow through the mountain, the solubility of key isotopes in that water, localized barriers to prevent free access of water to the waste, and the dilution of waste once it reaches groundwater.

For limited amounts of water flowing past the waste, solubility is likely to limit the movement of radionuclides to groundwater, although it is possible that some radio-nuclides could be transported as colloids, particles less than a micron across suspended in liquids. Projections of performance out to a million years indicate that the peak dose to a hypothetical individual who drinks water from a well 25 kilometers from the repository would not occur until several hundred thousand years hence.

Red Herrings

In recent years, there have been a few controversies over the stability of a Yucca Mountain repository. The most sensational one concerned the potential for a

Living with High-Level Radioactive Waste

Created by nuclear fission, high-level radioactive waste comes from two different sources: the commercial generation of nuclear power, as well as the production of plutonium for nuclear weapons.

Commercial and military wastes differ in several respects, which are relevant to their long-term safety in a repository. Military waste includes many different types, among them spent fuel. By far the largest component of defense waste is the reprocessing residue stored in underground tanks at the Hanford complex in Washington State and at the Savannah River site in South Carolina. These wastes have had most of their plutonium and uranium extracted through chemical reprocessing; their current hazardous nature comes from the presence of other radioactive elements produced by fission. In contrast, spent commercial power-plant fuel contains substantial quantities of uranium and plutonium, in addition to fission products.

Because of these differences, military nuclear wastes will decay to a safe level more rapidly than spent fuel will. For spent fuel or military waste that has been stored for more than a decade, the dominant radionuclides at the time of disposal are cesium 137 and strontium 90, both with half-lives of around 30 years. Initially, cesium and strontium generate most of the heat in a sample of waste and set the requirements for shielding to protect workers. After several centuries,

continued on following page

continued from previous page

the cesium and strontium will have decayed to levels that are too low to worry about.

After the strontium and cesium are gone, the fission product of concern in both spent fuel and defense waste is technetium 99, with a half-life of 211,100 years. Unlike high-level defense waste, spent fuel also contains americium 241 (with a 432.2-year half-life), carbon 14 (5,730 years), plutonium 239 (24,110 years), neptunium 237 (2.14 million years) and a variety of less important isotopes. Carbon 14 has received much attention because, unlike most other radioisotopes in the waste, it could be released directly from the repository as gaseous carbon dioxide.

A second major difference between the two wastes is their physical form at the time of disposal. Before the Department of Energy's tank wastes are put into a repository, highly radioactive components will be separated from the bulk of the tank wastes, vitrified (melted with other ingredients to make glass) and poured into stainless-steel cans. The Hanford wastes are expected to produce between 10,000 and 60,000 of these glass "logs," each 3 meters long by two thirds of a meter in diameter.

Commercial spent fuel consists of the fuel itself, which is a uranium dioxide ceramic, encased in a zirconium alloy fuel cladding. For disposal in a repository, assemblies of these fuels will be fitted into large waste canisters. —C. G. W.

nuclear criticality—that is, a self-sustaining nuclear chain reaction—as the waste dissolved and migrated through the mountain. Another one was related to the potential for groundwater to rise up and engulf the repository.

Both of these hypothetical situations have been addressed at length elsewhere. My view, briefly, is that they are technical "red herrings." While the possibility of criticality at some time far into the simple technical fixes could render its probability negligible. The simple addition of depleted uranium to waste canisters would be one such approach. If wastes were contained long enough for the plutonium 239 to decay to uranium 235, the depleted uranium would prevent a criticality. This process would take quite a while; plutonium 239 has a half-life of 24,110 years. The depleted uranium would, in effect, prevent the plutonium from becoming concentrated enough to go critical.

The possibility of groundwater reaching the repository level at Yucca Mountain also seems a very small concern. A National Academy of Sciences committee studied the issue in detail and concluded that there were no plausible mechanisms that could cause the water table to rise to such an extent and that there was no physical evidence that this had ever occurred before.

Although these two concerns may not seem to have much merit in and of themselves, they do underscore the uncertainty inherent in any analytical projection so far into the future. For a Yucca Mountain repository, even the phrase "far into the future" is ambiguous;

it can be taken to mean 10,000 or as many as one million years.

Experiments may be conducted to generate input for models of how a repository might behave, but predictions of very long-term behavior from short-term tests are always suspect. Unfortunately, few, if any, experiments could feasibly be done to provide a basis for the long-term projections required to assess repository performance for the practical life of the waste.

One of the very few such efforts so far uses natural analogues such as deposits of uranium ore to predict repository performance. Because the major component of spent fuel is uranium, and because plutonium 239 decays to uranium, the behavior of uranium in a natural setting is relevant to how a repository might perform. The fact that such ore deposits have existed for many millions of years without dissolving away provides evidence that, at least in some geologic settings, it is possible to isolate such materials over extended timescales. But what is not known is how many uranium deposits have not survived.

Hazy Future

The Yucca Mountain project has an uncertain future. Officially, if the DOE determines that Yucca Mountain is a suitable place to build a repository, the department will apply to the U.S. Nuclear Regulatory Commission for a license to construct and operate one there. If the commission grants the license, the state of Nevada can refuse the project, but the rejection can be overridden by a congressional vote.

It may never even make it that far, however. Although the investigatory and exploratory phase of the Yucca Mountain project is already almost a decade old, the anticipated time when a repository could be ready to receive nuclear waste is no closer than it was when work began. This year's federal financial allocation, $315 million, is about half of what was requested, and 1,100 fewer people are working on the project than a year ago. The most effective congressional supporter of a radioactive waste repository, Senator J. Bennett Johnston of Louisiana, has announced his plans to retire after this term.

The forces in the early 1980s that gave rise to the present policy were an unusual alignment of nuclear power industry and environmental group interests. The electric utility industry wanted to implement waste disposal rapidly, so that this critical obstacle to the rebirth of nuclear power was removed, and the environmentalists' desire was to ensure that spent reactor fuel was not reprocessed and that the proliferation threat that they associated with plutonium recycling and breeder reactors be avoided.

From the present perspective, these motivations and objectives seem almost irrelevant. Nuclear power has many problems, of which waste disposal is only one. Were the waste problem settled tomorrow, orders for new U.S. power reactors are unlikely for many economic reasons. Similarly, the hundreds of metric tons of bomb-grade plutonium released by the post–cold war decommissioning of nuclear weapons in the U.S. and former Soviet Union has made concerns about spent power-reactor fuel as a proliferation threat seem insignificant. The DOE is gathering nearly 100 metric tons of plutonium from decommissioned nuclear weapons and from other sources; no decisions have been made on its ultimate disposition, but the issue will likely overlap somehow with policies for managing spent nuclear fuel and high-level nuclear waste.

Significant though they are, such issues should not be permitted to distract attention from the basic facts. Storage of spent nuclear fuels above ground is an economic and technically proven interim measure. But such a measure is not up to the task of safely and efficiently securing dangerous materials that will exist for thousands of years to come.

The Author

Chris G. Whipple is a vice president of ICF Kaiser, an environmental engineering, remediation and consulting company. He was chairman of the National Academy of Sciences's Board on Radioactive Waste Management and now heads the Environmental Protection Agency's advisory committee on the Waste Isolation Pilot Plant, a nuclear waste repository in New Mexico. He is a member of the National Council on Radiation Protection and Measurement and was one of the founders of the Society for Risk Analysis.

Groundwater in the land can release pollution into the air, potentially making people sick. This happens when the groundwater is polluted and that groundwater moves up through the soil into building foundations and homes. Eventually, pollution in the water evaporates into the air and we breathe it into our lungs. Scientists call this occurrence vapor intrusion.

The following article is about some very common pollutants and suspected carcinogens in vapor intrusion: chlorinated solvents. They are not uncommon, but they are very hard to measure indoors. You can't just measure the air in a house because the air changes frequently and may already have high levels of vapor intrusion pollutants, such as air fresheners and paints. The preferred method for indoor measurement of vapor intrusion is the use of a computer model to predict pollution levels.

A model is a set of complicated equations in a computer. Scientists can insert known values into a computer model (such as the amount of moisture in soil) and calculate what level of pollution to expect. Such models are used for all sorts of predictions in science, including predictions of climate, earthquakes, and animal populations.

This article explains some of the problems in using computer models to predict levels of pollution from vapor intrusion and explains

*why regulators have not yet devised a way to
assess contaminated sites. —KW*

"A Case of the Vapors"
by Rebecca Renner
Scientific American, July 2002

Denver, the mile-high city, has a deep down problem.
Underneath a neighborhood in the southeastern part
of town lies a groundwater plume contaminated with
chlorinated solvents. Such contamination is not
unusual; chlorinated organic solvents, many of them
dry-cleaning and degreasing agents, are among the most
common and troublesome groundwater contaminants
in the U.S. But in Denver, potentially harmful concentrations of these volatile compounds—all suspected
carcinogens—have accumulated in houses by moving
up through the soil and foundations, in a phenomenon
known as vapor intrusion.

Denver's case, which has led to the installation of
fans and venting systems in more than 350 homes, is
at the heart of a vigorous national debate among
environmental scientists about the prevalence and
significance of this problem. Federal and state site
managers are charging that the U.S. Environmental
Protection Agency's assessments, which are based on
theoretical modeling, substantially underestimate the
amount of contamination in houses.

Vapor intrusion is still a new concern for regulators,
and evaluating this pollution pathway is a can of worms.

Directly measuring the levels is usually not the best way to do it, explains environmental consultant Christopher VanCantfort, because indoor air changes so frequently. Worse, many houses already have background levels of chlorinated organic solvents—emitted by household air fresheners, paints and glues—that exceed health guidelines, says Lance Wallace, an EPA research scientist.

Indoor measurement difficulties are one of the reasons modeling is the most widely accepted approach for evaluating vapor intrusion. But the popular model is complex and, some claim, misused. The method, developed in 1991 by Shell chemical engineers Paul Johnson and Robbie Ettinger, breaks down volatile intrusion into several steps. First, contaminants volatilize out of groundwater. Then they diffuse through soil toward a building. Once near the foundation, the lower internal pressure sucks the contaminants into the building through cracks and other openings.

Johnson and Ettinger's model is good, but it is complicated to use. A contaminated-site manager needs to plug in much information about the soil and its subsurface structure. "Most of the model inputs are things that you don't usually measure in a site assessment," says Johnson, who is now at Arizona State University. "My experience is that model misuse is a significant problem among regulators, industry and consultants," he concludes. For example, roughly half a dozen states currently list levels of chlorinated solvents in groundwater that could cause vapor intrusion problems in houses. But the levels are "all over the map," VanCantfort observes. The reason for the discrepancies, which can be as high as 1,000-fold, is that states use slightly different variations of the same model and different default values for important factors, such as soil type and soil moisture.

But others question whether it is even possible to come up with the right numbers to plug in: VanCantfort notes that the model has not been adequately field-tested. Michigan's Environmental Science Board expressed similar unease. "With this model, it's all too possible to decide that a site is safe when in fact it's risky, or risky when in fact it is safe," VanCantfort insists.

Vapor intrusion may also be coming in for intense scrutiny because the hazard can result in tough cleanup numbers. "Most people believe that drinking-water standards are the most stringent standards for ground-water," explains Paul Locke, a scientist with the Massachusetts Department of Environmental Protection. "But in reality, vapor infiltration for chlorinated hydrocarbons" requires stricter control. More communities may be getting the vapors unless regulators devise a better way to evaluate contaminated sites.

Rebecca Renner is based in Williamsport, Pa.

4 Life

Life in the Amazon rain forest of Brazil is dense and diverse. Scientists estimate that there are between 2 million and 30 million species in the Amazon rain forest—making it biologically valuable because about 50 percent of the world's plants and animals live there. In addition, the rain forest is economically valued for its hardwood (mahogany), medicinal plants, tourism, and land for farming. The question is, how can the Amazon be protected while providing a profit for the country?

This article is about balancing the demands on the Amazon rain forest: what we know about the forest, what some researchers are doing in the forest, and how the Brazilian people are involved in both using and conserving the forest. One scientist, Barbara L. Zimmerman, is working to set up a research station and a preserve on native land in the southern Amazon, with the hopes of bringing more scientists, tourists, and profit to the country. Others are working to understand how big a chunk of forest is needed *to sustain its biodiversity. Still others are looking for ways to rehabilitate tracts of forests that were previously used for cattle and farming.*

In the end, the biologists studying the Amazon have become administrators for conservation projects, and the author suggests there may still be a way for humans and nature to survive together. —KW

"Sustaining the Amazon"
by Marguerite Holloway
Scientific American, July 1993

Big, brown and sedate, two toads blink in the beam of the flashlight, while nearby pairs of green "eyes," the phosphorescent markings of click beetles, move lazily along the leaf-laden floor of the forest. On this night, Barbara L. Zimmerman is trying to find what she calls "the ultimate frog" for a group of visitors she is accompanying through the dark tangle of the Brazilian rain forest. The tropical biologist can hear her quarry's barklike call, but the vivid emerald creature, *Phyllomedusa bicolor*, is nowhere to be seen.

Instead the nocturnal search reveals the red irises of *P. tarsius*, the penultimate green tree frog; *Plica plica*, a mint-chocolate-chip-colored lizard; the two enormous, poisonous toads, *Bufo marinus*; as well as a tireless, resonant frog, *Osteocephalus taurinus*, that resides in the camp's drainpipe. The Amazon is like this: look for one thing, find another.

Zimmerman, who formerly stalked frogs in this forest 70 kilometers north of the city of Manaus to study their mating patterns, now pursues them primarily for pleasure. These days, her research centers on people, a shift in emphasis that is increasingly common in the Amazon. She has come here this time as part of a team of tropical scientists who are reviewing a project as well as possibilities for collaborative studies. Inevitably, their discussions turn to ways of reconciling the preservation of the rain forest with economic development.

Many of the scientists seem resigned to the prospect that the rain forest will, in large part, be cut down even as they struggle to understand the biological wealth of this tropical ecosystem. The five million square kilometers of Amazon tree cover make up the largest continuous expanse of tropical rain forest remaining in the world. Although such forests cover only 7 percent of the planet's land surface, they are inhabited by some 50 percent of the plants and animals found on the globe (estimates of which range from a total of two million to 30 million species). Most disturbing of all is the fact that nobody really knows how many. But as many as 27,000 species may be consigned to extinction every year, calculates Harvard University biologist Edward O. Wilson. This destruction is the result of forests being felled at a rate of 1,800 hectares (about 4,500 acres) every hour.

The impact of these extinctions is multifold: the rain forests have profound philosophical, spiritual, cultural, scientific and economic significance. Because

Brazil is considered to have the highest species diversity on the earth, it is the epicenter of efforts to stem deforestation. So far the country has lost only an estimated 12 percent of its forest, a sign of hope to many researchers and development experts. Yet the country has a debt burden of $121 billion, staggering poverty and one of the most unequal distributions of wealth in the world. Any successful attempt to preserve the forest must necessarily meet human economic objectives.

By working with the people who live in and use the forest—including Indians, rubber tappers, ranchers, loggers, farmers and industrialists—scientists such as Zimmerman hope to strike a balance between extremes of conservation and exploitation that will protect species and threatened environments while fostering economic development and reducing poverty. "Do what you can do—just do something," urges Don E. Wilson, head of the biodiversity program at the Smithsonian Institution.

These efforts are among the myriad attempts to implement what is called sustainable development. The idea was the linchpin of the 1992 United Nations Conference on Environment and Development, but the fashionable phrase, which now appears in nearly every grant or loan application, is still being defined. Thus, researchers are seeking pieces of a mosaic of development, the overall pattern of which, like the web of biodiversity, can only be guessed at.

Slowly, however, some scientific underpinnings for sustainable development appear to be emerging. Sometimes the answers seem to contravene assumptions

Amazon rain forest extends into nine countries and covers 60 percent of Brazil—some 510 million hectares (about 1.3 billion acres).

about what might be ecologically sustainable. Scientists are investigating how to use the millions of hectares of formerly productive pasture that lie abandoned throughout the Amazon. Once cut down, the rain forest does not necessarily become a desert but rather a field or a secondary forest that can again be harnessed for ranching, logging or agriculture. If this land can be returned to productivity, it would reduce pressure to cut virgin forest. Indeed, a group of researchers recently challenged dogma by suggesting that cattle ranching—long thought to be an ecological and economic anathema—may be a viable land use.

Whatever the project or finding, controversy is never far off in Brazil. The country is so vast and the economic, social and political problems so complicated that every issue is labyrinthine: follow the thread, and there are often several Minotaurs. One of the most contentious topics involves the future of indigenous people and their land. It is on one of these Indian reserves, with a people called the Kayapó, that Zimmerman has chosen to work.

Zimmerman and her sponsors—the environmental group Conservation International and the David Suzuki Foundation, a Canadian nonprofit organization—are setting up a scientific research station on remote Kayapó territory in the southern reaches of the Amazon. The villagers of Aukre, which means "place where the river bottom is noisy," have set aside 5,000 hectares for the field station within the 500,000 hectares of rain forest that they control.

The project will characterize the biodiversity of a region that has not been extensively studied, Zimmerman explains. The flora and fauna of the Amazon vary so greatly that adjacent sites can shelter entirely different species. One hectare in the eastern Amazon may have 120 tree species, whereas a nearby hectare may have 170. The woods around Aukre may have creatures or plants that are not found, or are infrequently seen, elsewhere in Brazil.

Many scientists have shied away from working with Indians because the issues facing them are so volatile. "It is a land mine," comments Anthony B. Anderson, program officer at the Ford Foundation in Brazil. "There are politics within the tribes and without, as well as all of these misconceptions about what the Indians are supposed to be."

The debate about what indigenous people should do with their land is bitter. As many as 79 million hectares have been or are in the process of being designated as reserves, according to Stephan Schwartzman of the Environmental Defense Fund. To many scientists and environmentalists, this expanse represents a perfect series of places to preserve and study biodiversity as well as native cultures. The Kayapó, for instance, control 10 million hectares, a region approximately the size of Ontario.

Yet these lands are also rich in minerals and timber and so are ripe for economic development. Many are illegally infiltrated by loggers and gold miners, such as the territory of the Yanomami in northern Brazil, where violence, disease and mercury poisoning, the last a result of the gold extraction process, are pervasive. But the fierce reputation of Kayapó warriors has successfully deterred encroachments. Some Kayapó chiefs have opted to sell mahogany and mining rights, a decision that has aggravated environmentalists. Greenpeace, the international environment group, recently sought to enforce a ban on mahogany logging on the tribal lands— an action that has, in turn, aggravated certain Kayapó.

It is estimated that about 40 percent of the Amazon's mahogany trees—which, in general, only grow in a strip across the lower portion of the rain forest—thrive on reserves.

Noble Savage

Development experts and conservationists, many of whom struggle to help establish reserves, expect that Indians should maintain the rain forest intact. This view has been shaped, in part, by anthropological studies documenting tribes' sustainable use of the forest and their sophisticated agricultural systems. Others experts argue, however, that sustainability has been achieved by default: the forest is large enough to recover from alteration, and populations are small enough to have limited impact. "The idea of the noble savage has really confused the issue," Anderson notes. "Indians, like everyone else, are opportunistic. In the past, they used resources sustainably, but not always."

If Zimmerman's project is successful, it could help settle the debate by supplying a source of income for Indians while simultaneously maintaining biodiversity. Aukre is an interesting choice for such a site because it has experienced each facet of the controversy. The village's chief, Paiakan, is famous as a spokesperson for protecting rain forests and tradition, as well as for being a skillful politician who could unify previously warring tribes in the face of developers. Yet other villagers have disagreed with his view. In addition, Paiakan can no longer easily be an advocate for indigenous people in the Amazon: he has reportedly been charged with attempted rape and is awaiting trial.

The region around the reserve is as scarred as the tribe. The flight northwest from Redenção—a frontier town whose economy is based on minerals and mahogany from Kayapó land—to Aukre offers a view of the entire spectrum of development. Ranches, logged plots and rivers disfigured by gold miners are slowly replaced by uninterrupted forest. On the ground, the new research site appears intact, although it is bordered on one side by an old logging road. The station stands in the middle of a clearing just off a river, an hour by canoe from Aukre. Bright-blue morpho butterflies flit down trails pockmarked with tapir tracks, and the wolf whistle of screaming pia birds rings out from the canopy.

Zimmerman intends to fill this place with graduate students and researchers who will study the forest and work with the Kayapó. She notes that natives have a different way of knowing the forest—for instance, men called *mateiros* can identify hundreds of trees by smell alone. She expects that such collaboration will yield medicinal plants or new crops and perhaps a strategy for the sustainable harvesting of mahogany.

In turn, the project is expected to bring income to Aukre. Scientists will buy local products, ecological tours may visit the site under Zimmerman's stewardship and fly-fishermen may explore the river's varied population of fish. Collaborative studies with the Kayapó could also lead researchers to medicinal plants or agricultural techniques that bring some financial return. Although the town makes money harvesting Brazil nut oil for Body Shop International, a British company that develops and sells natural beauty products, it is not enough.

The fervor about the future of Indian lands is echoed in arguments about another kind of reserve: extractive reserves. These areas—which are also set aside by the government and whose boundaries are also rarely enforced—are places where local people harvest natural products, including latex, palm hearts and Brazil nuts, without damaging the rain forest. Such reserves were made famous by Francisco Alves Mendes Filho, known as Chico Mendes, a rubber tapper from the town of Xapuri in the western state of Acre. Because of his efforts to organize the rubber tappers to fight for their land, Mendes was murdered by cattle ranchers in 1988.

Extractive reserves, of which there are now 14 covering a total of three million hectares, confer land rights to squatters and people whom large landholders have dispossessed. (In Brazil, 4.5 percent of the land-owners control 81 percent of the farmland.) The presence of these powerful ranchers is felt for the entire four-hour drive from the city of Rio Branco to Xapuri. The road is flanked by pastures, and the landscape is verdant but eerie: ghostlike Brazil nut trees, lone relics of the forest, stand in the green fields, their bleached branches luminous against the backdrop of dark, stormy sky. A law prohibits cutting these majestic trees, but once pasture is burnt around them, the Amazon sun inevitably desiccates them.

Disagreements about extractive reserves pivot on questions of economic viability. Scientists on one side argue that insufficient markets exist for many of the products. By studying past market cycles, Alfredo Kingo Oyama Homma of the Brazilian Enterprise for Agricultural Research (EMBRAPA) found that when a forest product such as latex becomes commercially important it is inevitably introduced into higher yielding plantations; in 1991 about 60 percent of Brazil's natural rubber came from plantations. Or the material is made synthetically. As a result, the price plummets, and small-scale extraction ceases to be profitable.

Other researchers counter that the matter has not been settled. One study conducted in Peru several years ago found that 72 products could be harvested from a one-hectare plot for an annual yield of $422. The investigators concluded that this approach was more lucrative than the one-time logging profit of $1,000. On the other hand, Anderson notes, "if you took a random sample of forests here in the Amazon, you would not find many that would have such a high value of nontimber forest products." In addition, the Peruvian products could be marketed regionally, a situation that does not yet exist for many of the reserves in the Amazon.

Nevertheless, Anderson and others argue that there may be a compromise. "I am one of the proponents, so I am suspect, " Anderson cautions. "But I like to think that I am somewhere in the middle ground. Maybe the term 'extractive reserve' is a misnomer. These are areas zoned to protect the rights of people who live in the forest." Anderson explains that once land claims are guaranteed, extractivists begin to look for supplemental livelihoods—such as raising livestock or planting additional crops. Extraction "is undergoing a transformation, and therefore it is potentially a basis for sustainable development." The implications of this economic diversification for the preservation of bio-diversity are not yet established.

Many scientists and nongovernmental organizations—Cultural Survival, a Boston-based group of anthropologists, and the New York Botanical Garden's Institute for Economic Botany, among them—are working with rubber tappers and Brazil nut gatherers to find other products, such as medicinal plants and fruits, and to open new markets. Some are addressing the overwhelming problems of communication and transportation. Many individuals who harvest forest products travel for days to sell them.

Getting out of Xapuri, even at the outset of the rainy season, illustrates the challenge of reaching the market. Gomercindo Clovia Garcia Rodrigues, a member of the extractivist cooperative of Xapuri, hitches a ride with a group of travelers back to Rio Branco so he can visit his dentist—he says he was shot in the jaw by ranchers a while ago, and the wound continues to hurt. As he describes the woes of driving at this time of year, the white Fiat sinks in the red muck of the road, for the first time. After the fourth escape, we are covered with a thick, rust-colored patina of mud. The windshield wiper breaks, the rain blinds and the battery fails. Rodrigues laughs: the Amazon has made his point.

Amazon Microcosm

At the opposite end of the country, in the eastern state of Pará, researchers are working with Rodrigues's traditional foes: ranchers and loggers. In a valley capped by smoke, fires from dozens of sawmills smolder. The black and gray plumes hang in the humid air of a late afternoon. The only motion is that of children playing alongside the barren road, tin cans tied to the bottoms of their feet like shiny platform shoes.

Although the image of a deforested Amazon is by now a familiar one, a close look at this landscape reveals an unusual collaboration. Christopher Uhl of Pennsylvania State University, Daniel C. Nepstad of the Woods Hole Research Center and Adalberto Verissimo, Paulo Barreto and their colleagues at the Amazon Institute of Man and the Environment (IMAZON) are working with owners and employees at local sawmills and farms. They are documenting ways of reclaiming land that has been abandoned and of managing forests for timber. Uhl and Verissimo are fond of describing the region near the town of Paragominas, where they have focused their effort, as a microcosm for the Amazon. They believe that if the forces driving deforestation are understood and altered here, the lessons can be applied to states such as Rondônia and Mato Grosso, which, by 1988, had both lost some 24 percent of their forest.

Pará encompasses one third of the Brazilian Amazon and had lost 13 percent of its forest cover by 1990. The area opened for development in the mid-1960s, when completion of a highway connected the city of Brasília to Belém, the hub of Brazil's rubber boom. At that time, the government promoted cattle herding by offering subsidies—often as great as 75 percent of the costs of starting the ranch—to settlers. The government also offered property to anyone who could demonstrate that they had cleared land, a policy that led to spasms of deforestation.

Several problems quickly emerged. Because the forest covets its nutrients, its soils are relatively poor. Although ranchers slashed and burned the forest, releasing phosphorus, nitrogen, potassium and other riches into the ground, the infusion was short-lived. After a few seasons of overgrazing, grasses no longer grew. A riot of unruly and, to cattle, unappetizing vegetation soon covered the fields. By the 1980s ranching was not economically worthwhile. The government proved as unsupportive as the soil. A fiscal crisis dried up subsidies, making clear-cutting and cattle raising even less attractive.

A new industry emerged in ranching's stead. The native forests of southern Brazil had by then been for the most part leveled, and ranchers realized they could afford to rejuvenate degraded pastures by selling logging rights to their property. More than 100 species of wood, which had been viewed as impediments to pasture, were harvested. By 1990 there were 238 sawmills near Paragominas.

Today logging is the area's principal industry, and it is just as unsustainable as ranching was. IMAZON researchers have determined that for each tree that is removed in a process called selective logging, 27 other trees that are 10 centimeters or more in diameter are severely injured, 40 meters of road are created and 600 square meters of canopy are opened. Recovery of the forest is slow even under these conditions: it can take 70 years for selectively logged forests to resemble their original state.

Nevertheless, Verissimo, Uhl and others think sustainable approaches to logging and ranching are possible. "I am much more optimistic than I was five years ago," Verissimo comments as he bounces in a car on the way to a ranch, Fazenda Vitória. At the study station there, he climbs a tower that stands at the intersection of the four distinct kinds of land that characterize the region: primary, or pristine, forest; partially regrown, or secondary, forest; pasture that is in use; and abandoned pasture. Verissimo points to the old pasture, explaining that the forest is slow to invade such sites, in part, because some seed-dispersing birds do not venture into open spaces.

Although there are about 10 million hectares of abandoned pasture in the Brazilian Amazon, scientists are just beginning to monitor what happens to land once it has been burned, grazed and then left. The investigations support one of the most exciting possibilities for sustainable development. If already deforested areas could be efficiently used for agriculture, ranching or logging, pressure could be taken off the primary rain forest. "There is no need to deforest when two thirds of the already deforested land is not being used in a reasonable way," Uhl notes.

Alternatively, if such lands could be restored or coaxed back into forest, biodiversity could be better protected. Understanding which trees, plants and creatures reestablish themselves first and under what conditions could allow researchers to speed up the recovery. Uhl cautions, however, that making the process economically attractive is critical. "Restoration makes us all feel good, but it doesn't necessarily address the key issue," he warns. "Putting money into it without economic development is not the best thing to do."

Studies of pastures and ranching have already led Uhl and his colleague Marli M. Mattos of Woods Hole to the somewhat heretical conclusion that, under certain conditions, cattle ranching can be profitable. They observe that if ranchers manage abandoned land intensively—that is, by introducing fertilizer or by planting better adapted species—cattle herds for beef and for dairy products can be lucrative. In fact, ranchers could increase their profits as much as fivefold at the same time that employment could rise. (Given estimates of population in Brazil—246 million by 2025—considerations of employment are fundamental.)

The two scientists note that the drawbacks to intensive ranching are significant. "Fire is becoming more and more common," Uhl states. "It will increase as landscapes are altered. The high forest is by nature quite resilient to fire, but as soon as you begin to alter it, it is much more prone to burning." According to Nepstad of Woods Hole, more than one half of the land in an 80-kilometer radius around Paragominas burned in 1992.

There are other ecological costs as well. Nepstad has shown in studies of soil and root systems that pastures hold only 3 percent of the aboveground carbon and 20 percent of the root carbon that forests do. Moreover, some 220 tons of carbon are released when the slash from each hectare of forest is burned. This emission has implications for global warming: tropical forest loss is estimated to have contributed one quarter of the carbon released into the atmosphere during the past decade.

Evapotranspiration—the means by which roots absorb water from the soil and release it—is also reduced in pasture because the root systems are relatively shallow and cannot reach deep deposits of moisture. In the Amazon, where 50 percent of precipitation may be generated by the flora, changes in evapotranspiration could cause alterations in local climate and rainfall patterns that adversely affect agriculture. Reductions in rainfall, in turn, cause the local temperature to increase, hampering vegetation and crops.

The ranching conclusions reveal some of the problems of defining the word "sustainable." "It is a really tricky term. There are all sorts of ways to measure sustainability, from an environmental, an ecological and a social perspective. It is a rare land use indeed that could fulfill all three criteria," observes Anderson of the Ford Foundation. "Don't get me wrong, I am not saying ranching is good, but it is not necessarily as bad as it seemed in the earlier literature. The question is not whether or not ranching is suitable, because it is there to stay."

Research on sustainable logging in Paragominas is not as controversial. In a forested site adjacent to the study tower, IMAZON's Barreto describes one simple strategy he has designed to help combine forest management and profit. Loggers routinely send workers into the forest to mark and cut the prize trees. Equipment then follows and creates roads. Barreto has found that by plotting the chosen trees in a simple software program, a shorter—and therefore less destructive and less expensive—network of roads can be designed.

In addition, injury to the surrounding trees can be reduced by as much as 30 percent. Pruning vines in a selectively logged forest can also permit light to reach seedlings, accelerating the growth of commercially important species. If loggers implemented these two techniques, Barreto says, forests would take 35 instead of 70 years to reach their prelogged stature. "It would reduce their profits only slightly to get sustainability," Verissimo asserts.

Because internal and external demand for Amazonian timber is expected to grow, more research on forest management strategies is needed. In 1976, 14 percent of the country's sawn wood came from the rain forest; by 1986 the share had grown to 44 percent.

The number of wood processors grew from about 100 in 1952 to more than 3,000 in 1992. Unlike domestic demand, however, international demand may catalyze changes in logging practices. Currently less than 5 percent of the world's supply of tropical hardwood comes from Brazil, but supplies in Asia are plummeting. Yet "outside demand for timber could be quite positive if nongovernmental organizations are involved in promoting green labeling," Uhl says. "Retailers want to know where this wood is coming from. This little step is tremendously important."

Regardless of findings such as those in Paragominas, research amounts to nothing if it is not implemented. Because Brazil has no coherent Amazonian policy, the IMAZON workers and their colleagues have suggested that countywide plans would be effective. The Brazilian Constitution of 1988 conferred more power to counties; therefore, these local governments could enact legislation requiring that specified land be used intensively for pasture and logging. Such laws would generate jobs for the region and preserve primary forest. Uhl says ranchers and mill owners are beginning to implement aspects of this management strategy as they realize that resources are finite and that well-placed investments in intensification will help guarantee sustainability.

Survival, rather than profit, is the consideration behind another principal cause of deforestation. For impoverished farmers, shifting cultivation often provides the only source of livelihood, as the ubiquitous small, smoldering plots of trees alongside roads testify.

"Natural resources are the bleeding valve for the poor; that is where they turn to survive," observes Ralph M. Coolman, a tropical ecologist at North Carolina State University, who is currently working with EMBRAPA.

On the fields of an old water-buffalo ranch and former rubber and palm plantation near Manaus, Coolman and his colleagues are investigating agroforestry systems. Agroforestry combines animal husbandry with farming and forestry. The practice has a long history, but "scientific agroforestry is relatively new," says Erick C. M. Fernandes, also of North Carolina State and EMBRAPA. By determining which plants are best suited to particular soils, the researchers hope to be able to increase the subsistence and profit yield of shifting cultivars, while letting them stay indefinitely on the deforested land. They are identifying species that are best suited to fixing nitrogen and replacing other nutrients.

The effort to balance preservation and economics that characterizes the work of Fernandes and Coolman, the Paragominas group and Zimmerman's team can also be seen at one of the longest-running programs in the rain forest. This study, the brainchild of biologist Thomas E. Lovejoy, was created in 1979 as a collaboration between the National Institute for Amazon Research (INPA) and the World Wildlife Fund. Originally called the Minimum Critical Size of Ecosystems Project, it is now administered jointly by INPA and the Smithsonian Institution, where Lovejoy serves as assistant secretary for external affairs.

Business and Biodiversity

The program was established to answer a fundamental question of ecology: What is the smallest size an island (or, in this case, a tract of forest) can be and still maintain its biodiversity? The findings have direct implications for protecting species. Because landowners in the Amazon are required by law to retain 50 percent of their forests, scattered woods of all different sizes and shapes can be found everywhere, often surrounded by pasture.

By studying these various-sized plots and monitoring the changes in species composition, Lovejoy and his colleagues substantiated the prediction that larger forest fragments harbor more species than do smaller ones. But they also found that size alone was not always the determining factor. Instead it was crucial to understand the habitat requirements of each species. The project provided evidence that corridors—wooded paths that connect one fragment to another—facilitated the movement of certain species between fragments. Because it is hard to find large, uninterrupted parcels of land in many areas throughout the world, corridors are now incorporated in plans for wildlife preserves.

The project recently included an additional focus: the study of restoration, including the regrowth of pasture. Its new name, the Biological Dynamics of Forest Fragments Project, reflects this emphasis. Graduate students and researchers are expected to supply data for forest management, soil reclamation and commercial harvesting. The shift also ensured continued funding. According to tropical scientists, money for sustainable development is easier to obtain than are grants for basic research.

Lovejoy believes that another key to saving the rain forest lies in working with business. In the mid-1980s he developed the idea of debt-for-nature swaps. Recognizing that nations burdened with foreign debt could devote few resources to protecting ecology, Lovejoy proposed that conservation organizations repay a portion of the debt in exchange for a guarantee that land would be protected. Alleviating debt would both maintain biodiversity and strengthen the economy.

Building on this idea, Lovejoy and others are drawing attention to the financial importance of biodiversity. For example, pharmaceutical products, genetic stocks for agricultural products and timber species can be found in these forests. By publicizing this economic potential and the importance of conserving the resource base for future profit, Lovejoy says companies can be brought into the environmental loop—an approach that, he admits, is perceived with wariness on the part of many "green" organizations. Lovejoy, who in the course of one day easily moves from sitting on the dirt floor of a hut in a Kayapó village swatting blackflies to dining with the state's governor at a table dressed with crystal and silver, argues that sustainable development and the protection of biodiversity must be practiced at all levels of society.

To this end, he is advising the Brazilian Foundation for Sustainable Development, a consortium of 24 of the largest Brazilian companies, formed after the 1992 Earth Summit in Rio de Janeiro. The foundation plans to support research that will define sustainable development and to help companies act in environmentally sound ways. It will also finance the Forest Fragments Project. "Although the first step for sustainable development is in local communities, it is not only for them," says Angelo dos Santos, a foundation ecologist who has worked with INPA and Lovejoy. "Because of global climatic change, we need to work with big enterprises. We need a whole new approach."

At a December meeting at Camp 41—the "Tiffany" of sites at the Forest Fragment Project because of its ample hammocks and good cooks— Lovejoy, Zimmerman, Wilson and biologists from Brazil, Panama, Costa Rica, Peru and Mexico met to evaluate the project and to consider future studies. David B. Clark of La Selva Biological Station in Costa Rica pointed out that the only large tracts of forest left in his country are in parks. "I am trying to be philosophical about it," Clark says. "Most reserves in South America are going to be in this situation. Development is going to be right up against the protected areas."

As the scientists walked through the rain forest, noting differences and similarities between this region and those they study, it was apparent that no one was able any longer to devote attention exclusively to the study of biodiversity. "Many of us were not trained as administrators but as research biologists," the Smithsonian's Wilson comments. "Yet we find

ourselves, out of necessity, doing conservation work."
If they do it well enough, human beings and the rest
of Amazonian nature may yet find a way to survive
together. After all, in the Amazon you look for one
thing and keep finding others.

*Marguerite Holloway spent a month in the Brazilian rain
forest to report this article. Traveling from one end of the
Amazon basin to the other, she interviewed scientists
working at remote research stations, native preserves,
extractive reserves, ranches and frontier logging camps.*

*Life in tropical forests is often threatened when
those forests are harvested for their timber.
Because many tropical forests are located in
poor countries, where the value of the timber
sale often outweighs the value of the biodiversity,
such forests are slowly being destroyed.*

*In theory, a properly managed forest could
be harvested for its timber and replanted with
young trees that would grow to replace those
harvested. Over time, this would be a sustainable
forest. For something to be sustainable, it has
to be profitable now and profitable in the future.
If forests are simply harvested without being
replanted, the trees will eventually be gone and
the practice of harvesting will not be sustainable.*

*The next article is about possible ways to
conserve tropical rain forests and harvest them
at the same time. The authors have studied the
Amazonian rain forests of Bolivia and suggest
that sustainable forest management is not yet
possible. Instead, they recommend alternative
options. In the end—not surprisingly—money
is the deciding factor in which measures are
used. —KW*

"Can Sustainable Management
Save Tropical Forests?"
by Richard E. Rice, Raymond E. Gullison,
and John W. Reid
Scientific American, April 1997

To those of us who have dedicated careers to conserving
the biodiversity and natural splendor of the earth's
woodlands, the ongoing destruction of tropical rain
forest is a constant source of distress. These lush habitats
shelter a rich array of flora and fauna, only a small
fraction of which scientists have properly investigated.
Yet deforestation in the tropics continues relentlessly
and on a vast scale—driven, in part, by the widespread
logging of highly prized tropical woods.

   In an effort to reverse this tide, many conservationists have embraced the notion of carefully regulated
timber production as a compromise between strict
preservation and uncontrolled exploitation. Forest
management is an attractive strategy because, in theory,

it reconciles the economic interests of producers with the needs of conservation. In practice, sustainable management requires both restraint in cutting trees and investment in replacing them by planting seedlings or by promoting the natural regeneration of harvested species.

Most conservationists view this formula as a pragmatic scheme for countries that can ill afford to forgo using their valuable timber. We, too, favored this strategy until recently, when we reluctantly concluded that most of the well-meaning efforts in this direction by environmental advocates, forest managers and international aid agencies had a very slim chance for success. Although our concerns about the effectiveness of sustainable forestry have since mounted, our initial disillusionment sprang from our experiences trying to foster such practices in South America seven years ago.

A Disenchanting Forest

It was our interest in trying to preserve the Amazonian rain forests of Bolivia that brought two of us together for the first time in 1990, for a chance meeting at the bar of the sleepy Hotel El Dorado in downtown La Paz. Gullison had just arrived from Princeton University to conduct research on the ecology of mahogany (*Swietenia macrophylla* King), the most valuable species in the tropical Americas. Rice was about to return to Washington, D.C., after working with the Smithsonian Institution at the Beni Biosphere Reserve, located next to the Chimanes Permanent Timber Production Forest, a tract of half a million hectares in lowland Bolivia. In the mid-1980s the International Tropical Timber Organization selected the Chimanes Forest as a model site for sustainable management, and we were both eager to help that program advance.

Although our first exchange over beer in La Paz was brief, by the end of the conversation we had agreed to collaborate further. Within a year we secured funding for what eventually became a four-year study. At the outset, our intention was for Gullison to establish how best to manage mahogany production from an ecological standpoint and for Rice to develop the economic arguments needed to convince timber companies to adopt policies based on these scientific findings.

As time passed, Gullison and his Bolivian field crew made steady progress in understanding the ecology of the forest. Mahogany seedlings, it turned out, grew and prospered only after sizable natural disturbances. In the Chimanes region, younger mahogany trees stood only near rivers where floods had recently swept the banks clear and buried competing vegetation under a thick blanket of sediment. Such disturbances in the past had created widely dispersed pockets where seedlings could grow, eventually producing groups of trees of approximately uniform age and size. For the problem at hand, this aspect of the ecology of mahogany was quite alarming: it meant that uncontrolled logging would invariably obliterate the older stands, where nearly all trees would be of a marketable size.

Those worries were exacerbated by the realization that there would be little natural growth to replace harvested trees even if the loggers cut the forest sparingly. Mahogany seedlings (and those of certain other tropical tree species) cannot grow under the shady canopy of dense tropical forest. With natural regeneration unlikely to prove adequate, human intervention would be needed to maintain the mahogany indefinitely.

How could a helping hand be provided? In theory, loggers could create the proper conditions for new mahogany to grow by mimicking nature and clearing large openings in the forest. But the effort would be enormous, and judging from previous attempts elsewhere to do just that, costly periodic "thinnings" would be required to remove competing vegetation. Such efforts to sustain the production of mahogany could disturb so much forest that the overall conservation objectives would surely be compromised. Hence, winning the battle for mahogany might still lose the war to preserve biodiversity. Appreciation of this difficulty led us to question what exactly it was we were trying to achieve.

Money Matters

Just as Gullison was discovering the difficulties of regenerating mahogany, Rice was finding that timber companies working in the Chimanes Forest had no economic incentive to invest in sustainable management. This conclusion was not entirely surprising given global trends: less than one eighth of 1 percent of the world's tropical production forests were operating on a sustained-yield basis as of the late 1980s.

Logging, as typically practiced in the tropics, rapidly harvests the most highly valued trees. The number of species extracted may be as low as one (where there is a specialty wood, such as mahogany) or as high as 80 to 90 (where there is demand for a wide variety). Logging companies generally show little concern for the condition of residual stands and make no investment in regeneration. This attitude emerges, in part, as a matter of simple economics. In deciding whether to restrict harvests, companies face a choice between cutting trees immediately and banking the profits or delaying the harvest and allowing the stand to grow in volume and value over time. Economics, it seems, dictates the decision.

In choosing the first option, a company would harvest its trees as quickly as possible, invest the proceeds and earn the going rate of return, which can be measured by real, or inflation-adjusted, interest rates. Because risks are considerable and capital is scarce, real interest rates in developing countries are often much higher than in industrial countries. For example, real interest rates on dollar-denominated accounts in Bolivia have averaged 17 percent in recent years, compared with 4 percent in the U.S. Similarly high rates of interest are common in most countries in Latin America. Thus, companies that rapidly harvest their assets can invest their profits immediately and generate continuing high rates of return.

The benefits of delaying harvests, in contrast, are small. From 1987 to 1994, real price increases for mahogany averaged 1 percent a year, whereas the average annual growth in volume of commercial-size mahogany trees is typically less than 4 percent. This combination of slow growth rates and modest price increases means that mahogany trees (as well as most other commercial tree species in the American tropics) rise in value annually by at most 4 to 5 percent— about the same as would be earned by a conservative investment in the U.S. and much less than competitive returns in Bolivia.

The value of the trees left to grow, moreover, could easily plummet if wind, fire or disease destroyed them or if in the future the government restricted logging. Therefore, choosing to leave mahogany growing amounts to a rather uncertain investment—one that would provide, at most, a rate of return that is essentially the same as could be obtained by harvesting the trees and banking the profits safely. Like most other business-people, who are unwilling to make risky investments in developing countries unless offered considerably higher returns, loggers choose to cut their trees as quickly as they can.

After making a careful analysis of the economics of logging in the Chimanes region, we discovered that unrestricted logging is from two to five times more profitable than logging in a way that would ensure a continued supply of mahogany. From a purely financial perspective, then, the most rational approach to logging appears to be exactly what timber companies are doing—harvesting all the available mahogany first, avoiding investments in future harvests, and then moving on in sequence to all species that yield a positive net return. Adam Smith's invisible hand, it appears, reaches deep into the rain forest.

The incentives driving uncontrolled logging prove especially powerful in developing countries, where government regulation is, in general, quite weak. The national forest authority in Bolivia, for instance, receives annually less than 30 cents for each hectare of land it administers. (The U.S. Forest Service, in comparison, gets about $44.) With such slim support, government regulators in Bolivia are hard-pressed to counterbalance the financial rewards of cutting all the valuable trees at once, and it is no wonder that few timber companies there invest any effort to help the targeted species regenerate.

The Value of Sustainability

After spending some time in the Chimanes region of Bolivia, we decided to investigate how severely logging there had injured the local environment. We quickly found that, although clearly unsustainable for mahogany, the physical effects of logging on the forest as a whole have been relatively mild. Because only one or two mahogany trees grow in a typical 10-hectare plot, road building, felling and log removal disrupt less than 5 percent of the land. We estimate that current logging practice causes considerably less damage than some forms of sustainable management (which require more intensive harvests of a wider variety of species). Indeed, a more sustainable approach could well double the harm inflicted by logging.

Sustainability is, in fact, a poor guide to the environmental harm caused by timber operations. Logging that is unsustainable—that is, incapable of maintaining production of the desired species indefinitely—need not be highly damaging (although in some forests it is, especially where a wide range of species have commercial value). Likewise, sustainable logging does not necessarily guarantee a low environmental toll. Ideally, companies should manage forests in a way that is both sustainable for timber and minimally disturbing to the environment. But when forced to choose between unsustainable, low-impact logging and sustainable, high-impact logging, environmentalists should make sure they pick the option that best meets their conservation objectives. If the maintenance of biodiversity is of paramount importance—as we believe it should be—a low impact (albeit unsustainable) approach may be the preferable choice.

Yet the quest to sustain the yield of wood indefinitely has become a central theme in efforts to preserve tropical forests. And conservation-minded people have proposed several strategies to overcome the economic obstacles to sustainable forest management. Their approaches, however, often fail to distinguish between the profitability of logging existing forests and the profitability of investing in regeneration. In the absence of strong governmental control, both must be financially attractive to succeed.

Efforts to increase the utilization of lesser known tree species provide an informative example. Some advocates of sustainable management contend that boosting market demand for lesser known species will make it worthwhile to maintain a production forest that otherwise might be converted to farmland or rangeland. Yet there is nothing—such as faster growth or a brighter price outlook—to suggest that investments in regenerating these species will be any more attractive than investments in regenerating currently targeted species. Larger markets for secondary species may only increase the number of trees that are harvested unsustainably.

A parallel argument can be made with regard to secondary, or value-added, processing. Such processing (of logs into furniture or plywood) is often said to have the dual advantages of allowing the use of a wider variety of species while providing a stronger economic incentive to manage forests sustainably. In fact, the promotion of value-added processing in many countries has actually reduced their overall earnings (because large subsidies are needed to attract the necessary investment) while greatly increasing both the pace and scale of forest destruction.

Arguments promoting secure land tenure suffer from a similar limitation. Environmental advocates point to the lack of long-term access to timber resources as a major cause of unsustainable management. The commonsense argument favoring tenure security is that, without it, timber companies will be reluctant to invest in future harvests. Yet ensuring that companies are, in principle, able to benefit from nurturing forest growth does nothing to provide the practical financial incentives to foster such practices. More secure land tenure makes investments in regeneration possible for timber companies to consider; it does not, however, automatically make these investments economically worthwhile. In fact, rather than promoting investments in regeneration, more secure tenure may simply lower the risk of making larger investments in logging equipment, thus encouraging swifter liquidation of the resource.

This very issue brought Reid to our team in 1994. Rice had met Reid two years earlier in a torrential storm in the heart of the Petén, Guatemala's heavily forested northern province. Logging there had been suspended by government decree, but Guatemala's policymakers were considering turning large tracts of forest over to companies under contracts that would have endured for 25 years.

We agreed that such lengthy tenure for loggers probably would not solve the problems of unsustainable logging and an expanding agricultural frontier. It could, we feared, hurt the thousands of people who roam these woods in search of chicle latex (a gum), ornamental palm leaves and allspice—all valuable products for export. So when local authorities drafted a proposal to allow timber interests long-term concessions in hopes of promoting sustainable management, Rice called Reid to ask whether he would like to examine that policy in detail. Six weeks later the Guatemalan government had our report, which demonstrated the hefty cut in profits that companies would have to absorb to manage these forests sustainably. As a result, the plan was shelved, although pressure remains to turn the forest over to the logging industry.

Certifiably Green

Many people concerned with the future of the rain forest view timber certification, or "green labeling," as the prime means of providing the economic incentive needed to spur sustainable management. Such certification programs call for voluntary compliance with established environmental standards in exchange for higher prices or greater market access, or both. While experts debate whether certification actually leads to higher market prices, the more important question is whether the premiums consumers are willing to pay for certified products are sufficient to bring about the necessary changes. Our economic analysis of the Chimanes operations indicated that for valuable species such as mahogany, current patterns of unsustainable logging can be as much as five times as profitable as a more sustainable alternative. Yet consumers appear to be willing to spend, at most, 10 percent more for certified timber than the price they would pay for uncertified wood products. The gap is enormous.

Nevertheless, certification has the potential to be an important tool for forest conservation, as long as these efforts concentrate on low-cost modifications that are sure to reduce environmental damage (such as preventing loggers from hunting forest animals) rather than expensive changes that bring doubtful benefits. Although there is not yet broad consumer demand for certified wood, there does appear to be a growing niche that could be filled if the costs of being green are kept to a minimum. In the meantime, it would be best to avoid altering the economic incentives facing all logging operations, such as increasing tenure security or promoting lesser known species, simply to benefit the small number involved with certification. Without much broader acceptance of certification, such policies may only speed the degradation of tropical forests.

What to Do?

The management of tropical forests for sustainable timber production is unlikely to become a widespread phenomenon, at least in the near future. Contrary economic incentives, limited government control and a lack of local political support will consistently thwart the best efforts in that direction, particularly in developing countries. Environmentalists need to recognize this reality. Although we see no easy solutions, there are a few strategies that deserve greater attention.

One possibility is to provide timber companies with low-interest loans to fund regeneration and the protection of biodiversity. Logging that includes these activities is not sufficiently profitable at the high interest rates typical in developing countries, but it

Vive la Différence

Why protect tropical forests? For one, because they harbor most of the planet's biodiversity, an umbrella term for the variety of ecosystems, species and genes present. Scientists estimate that tens of millions of species exist, but they have described between only 1.4 and 1.5 million of them. Half the species identified so far live in tropical forests, yet biologists suspect the proportion could reach 90 percent if a full tally were ever accomplished.

Some examples help to put the biological abundance of tropical forests in proper perspective. In one study, a single hectare of rain forest in Peru was found to house 300 tree species—almost half the number native to North America. In another assay, scientists counted more than 1,300 butterfly species and 600 bird species living within one five-square-kilometer patch of rain forest in Peru. (The entire U.S. claims 400 butterfly species and just over 700 bird species.) In the same Peruvian jungle, Harvard entomologist Edward O. Wilson uncovered 43 ant species in a single tree, which he pointed out was about the same number as exists in all of the British Isles.

Such diversity of plant and animal life is important to humans because it is essential for creating food, medicines and raw materials. Wild plants, for example, contain the genetic resources needed to breed crops for resistance to pests and disease. And about 120 clinically

continued on following page

continued from previous page

useful prescription drugs come from 95 species of plants, 39 of which grow in tropical forests. What is more, botanists believe that from 35,000 to 70,000 plant species (most drawn from tropical forests) provide traditional remedies throughout the world. Take away the places where such species live, and myriad medicines become lost forever.

One means to protect biodiversity is the Convention on International Trade in Endangered Species (CITES)—the 1973 treaty that helped to keep elephants and gorillas from becoming extinct. Bolivia, which is second only to Brazil in mahogany exports, recently asked the U.S. to join it in gaining protection for mahogany (*Swietenia macrophylla* King) under the CITES accord. The proposal seeks to include mahogany among the items in Appendix 2 of the treaty, which would require countries to monitor their exports to ensure that international trade does not threaten the species. (Appendix 1 of the CITES treaty includes those species that are already endangered and prohibits their export for international trade.)

The U.S. Fish and Wildlife Service agreed in January to request protective measures for mahogany during the next CITES meeting in June. Although the full implications of this proposal remain unclear, we hope this action will focus much needed attention on the question of how best to conserve biodiversity in tropical forests that are being logged.　　　　—R. E. R., R. E. G. and J. W. R.

could become so if funded by cheaper capital, perhaps provided by development banks or conscientious investors.

Another option is to promote the preservation of large forested areas within and around timber concessions. Such set-asides would be relatively inexpensive to monitor and could aid substantially in the conservation of biodiversity. Rather than just keeping forest cover, such protected areas could maintain forest that had nearly its full complement of species and old-growth structure. Ideally, these lands should be contiguous with, or near, other intact forest. To minimize the cost, we suggest focusing on commercially inoperable areas, such as places too steep to log or forests that have been lightly logged in the past.

Although such set-asides may be among the less economically productive areas under their control, timber companies are likely to resist any restrictions at all on their movements. In Bolivia the government is addressing this difficulty by offering loggers a financial reward for preservation. Under a law that has just been approved, the Bolivian government will collect a flat tax (of around $1 per hectare a year) for logging privileges. Timber companies can, however, designate up to 30 percent of their concessions as off-limits to logging, and the lands thus specified will be exempt from taxation. This policy should encourage loggers to protect their commercially marginal lands, and it may soften their resistance to having other areas set aside for the protection of the environment.

Finally, in forests such as Chimanes, where uncontrolled logging is selective and settlement pressures are low, accepting some elements of the status quo may prove to be the best available option. As in many areas of the Bolivian lowlands, logging in Chimanes is almost certain to continue long after the mahogany has been exhausted. In fact, the current pattern of selective harvest of a large number of commercial species, one or two species at a time, is a process that in some areas could require decades to complete. The challenge facing conservationists under such circumstances is not so much to convince the timber companies to stay and log sustainably for the long run but rather to institute some form of protection for old-growth forests while the opportunity remains.

Environmentalists also need to remember that many threats to tropical forests would continue even if sustainable management were to become widely adopted. National agricultural policies, road development and colonization can each pose a far greater danger to tropical forests than unsustainable logging. Reducing the destruction caused by these forces could do much more for forest conservation than revamping current forestry practices.

Clearly, no single strategy will work indefinitely or for all forests. Our prescriptions (particularly for old-growth set-asides) might ultimately succumb to the same forces that now frustrate sustainable forest management. Over time, producers will have an ever greater incentive to enter currently uneconomic areas.

So, in the absence of determined government oversight, these alternatives, too, would fail just as surely as efforts to impose sustainable forestry. Our set-aside proposal differs, however, in that it delivers real and immediate environmental benefits by protecting old-growth forest. Furthermore, it relies on straightforward restrictions about where logging occurs rather than on complicated technical rules dictating how logging is to be done.

Although far from providing fully satisfying solutions, the measures we suggest may be the most realistic means to harmonize conservation with tropical timber extraction, until such time as political and economic change in the developing world brings a widespread demand for more effective protection of these majestic tropical forests.

The Authors

Richard E. Rice, Raymond E. Gullison and John W. Reid came to study the problems of tropical forests from quite different perspectives. Rice obtained a bachelor's degree in economics at Grinnell College and went on to earn a master's in economics and, in 1983, a doctorate in natural resources from the University of Michigan. He is currently the senior director of the resource economics program at Conservation International in Washington, D.C. After graduating from the University of British Columbia with a degree in zoology, Gullison studied ecology and evolutionary biology at Princeton University, where he completed a Ph.D. in 1995. He now teaches at the Imperial

College of Science, Technology and Medicine in London. Reid earned a master's degree in public policy at Harvard University before joining Conservation International in 1994. His work there focuses on natural resource economics and policy issues concerning conservation in the tropics.

Life in the Everglades is in trouble. Florida's slow-moving, shallow, and partially saltwater river, known to scientists as marshland or wetland, is about half the size that it used to be. And the Everglades once was as large as the state of Massachusetts. Before the 1950s, the Everglades was a 60-mile-wide (90.6-kilometer-wide) river that ran the entire length of Florida. Today, large swaths have been dried out, and the land has been developed. After much discussion, federal and state governments, along with private groups, are trying to restore the water flow and life of the ecosystem.

Among the creatures that inhabit the Everglades are birds, fish, and alligators. Of these, perhaps most impressive is the seventy-some species of birds that live there. But over the past fifty years, the number of wading birds has decreased by about 90 percent.

This article is about the Army Corps of Engineers' effort to increase water flow in the

Everglades to almost its original volume. Today, water flow in the Everglades is managed by the Corps carefully, and there is a comprehensive plan to restore the area. —KW

"Replumbing the Everglades"
by Mark Alpert
Scientific American, August 1999

There's a good reason why the Everglades is called the "River of Grass." Until the latter half of this century, water flowed down the Florida peninsula in a shallow, 60-mile wide sheet, slowly gliding south from Lake Okeechobee to Florida Bay. This sheet flow gave rise to a uniquely rich ecosystem, a freshwater marsh covered with sawgrass and teeming with fish, alligators and wading birds. But in the 1950s and 1960s, the Army Corps of Engineers built a web of canals and levees to prevent flooding and to drain large sections of the area for farming. The canals diverted water to the Atlantic Ocean and the Gulf of Mexico, shunting hundreds of billions of gallons away from the Everglades every year. The result was an environmental disaster: the marshland has now shrunk to about half its original size, and the number of wading birds has decreased by an estimated 90 percent.

For the past decade, federal and state officials have been struggling to put together a plan to save the Everglades. The lead agency in this effort is none other than the Army Corps, which is expected to submit its final report to Congress this summer. The agency has proposed a $7.8-billion, 20-year replumbing project that would tear down more than 240 miles of canals and levees and increase the water flow in the Everglades to nearly its original volume. But the Army Corps plan would not eliminate all the man-made barriers that compartmentalize the region. Under the proposal, water would be stored in reservoirs and underground aquifers and periodically released to mimic the marshland's historical wet/dry cycle.

Some scientists say the project will not even come close to returning the Everglades to its natural state. "The plan will maintain a managed, fragmented structure instead of restoring the natural system," says Stuart Pimm, an ecologist at the University of Tennessee who has studied the Everglades extensively. "We should just take out the damn dikes, for God's sake, and leave the area alone." Gordon Orians, an ecologist at the University of Washington, worries that the plan's environmental goals have been compromised by concerns over flood control and the need to supply water to Florida's burgeoning population. "If restoring the Everglades was the only problem, it wouldn't be that tough to do," he says. "But that's not the real world."

Earlier this year Pimm, Orians and other scientists persuaded Interior Secretary Bruce Babbitt to establish an independent panel to review the restoration plan. In April the Army Corps agreed to accelerate its timetable for removing some of the canals and levees;

environmentalists are still pushing for more concessions, but many acknowledge that the current plan is probably the best they can get. Charles Lee, senior vice president of the Florida Audubon Society, noted that eliminating every man-made barrier in the Everglades would flood many residential areas in southern Florida. "We'd have to move a lot of people, and that's not politically doable," Lee says.

Another major obstacle to the restoration of the ecosystem is the Everglades Agricultural Area, a 750,000-acre spread of farms and sugarcane fields just south of Lake Okeechobee. The agricultural area acts as a giant cork, blocking the flow of water to the Everglades. Environmental groups had wanted to revive the sheet flow by converting large portions of this agricultural area into reservoirs, but the U.S. was able to wrest only 60,000 acres from the sugar growers, who have fiercely resisted government attempts to acquire more land.

This acreage was not enough to store all the water needed to revitalize the Everglades, so the Army Corps came up with an alternative: pumping as much as 1.6 billion gallons a day into underground storage zones. The injected water would float above the denser saline water in the aquifer and could be pumped back to the surface during dry periods. Aquifer storage has been tested at sites in southern Florida, but the restoration plan calls for storage zones with 100 times the capacity of any current project. Many environmentalists worry that the technology just won't work on such a large scale. "That's one of our biggest concerns," Lee says. "The Army Corps doesn't have a well-developed backup plan in case aquifer storage doesn't live up to its potential."

Stuart Appelbaum, restoration chief for the Jacksonville district of the Army Corps, contends that the agency could deepen surface reservoirs if underground storage does not prove feasible. He emphasizes that the restoration plan is not "written in stone." If all goes smoothly, Appelbaum says, Congress will give its approval by the fall of next year.

For some Everglades species, however, that may be too late. The changes in water flow have devastated the breeding grounds of the Cape Sable seaside sparrow, which lives almost exclusively in the Everglades. The birds' nests have been flooded during the wet seasons, and much of their habitat has gone up in flames during the dry seasons. The number of Cape Sable sparrows has dropped from tens of thousands a few decades ago to about 3,000 today, and some fear the species is headed for extinction. Pimm says he has met tourists in Everglades National Park who were stunned by the losses to the region's wildlife. He blames the catastrophe on the flood-control system built by the Army Corps, and he is not yet convinced that the agency can now correct its own mistakes.

The Endangered Species Act (ESA) has protected life that is in danger of extinction since the law was enacted in 1973. Intended to provide endangered or threatened species with protection from extinction, the ESA has become a point of contention between landowners and conservationists. This is because if a species is listed under the ESA, private landowners with that species on their property are restricted on what they can do on their land by the federal government—a perceived intrusion on private property rights that doesn't go over well with some.

Because of the belief that the Endangered Species Act restricts private property rights, it is an issue many people feel strongly about. Critics say that efforts to do things like "modernize" the ESA are sometimes intended to weaken protection for listed species. But not always—you just have to read carefully.

This article is about an effort more than ten years ago to change the protections required for listed species. In 2000, shortly after this article was published, Congress placed a year-long moratorium on listing new species. (In 1998, new priorities were established to list species as endangered or threatened.) Today, although new endangered species are being listed by the U.S. Fish and Wildlife Service once again, the debate over updating the ESA continues with no end in sight. —KW

"Endangered Again"
by Tim Beardsley
Scientific American, October 1995

Property-rights advocates and champions of biodiversity are gearing up for what could be a decisive political battle over the fate of the 1973 Endangered Species Act (ESA). The act, which provides legal protections for species that the secretary of the interior lists as endangered or threatened, is a lightning rod in what has become an argument over landowners' rights and habitat conservation. A concerted effort is expected this fall in Congress to remove some of the ESA's strongest provisions.

Ecologists generally support the law, which proponents say has stabilized populations of several hundred species. Both the bald eagle, which was recently delisted, and the peregrine falcon, which is scheduled for delisting, have been brought back from the brink of extinction because of protection afforded under the ESA. The Ecological Society of America has declared the legislation to be "a powerful and sensible way to protect biological diversity."

The National Research Council also gave the act a benediction when it reported this spring that it is "based on sound scientific principles" and "has prevented the extinction of some species and slowed the declines of others." Indeed, the research council specifically endorsed one of the act's most divisive provisions: its protection for distinct populations of animals that might belong to the same subspecies. That approach was justified, the council said, because the populations could be evolutionarily unique.

But these subpopulations may not be so special in the eyes of Representative Don E. Young of Alaska. The defenders of the ESA expect Young to introduce into the House an authorization bill that would defang it. The legislation would give the secretary of the interior the power to change the protections required for a listed species—thereby opening up what should be a science-based recovery plan to political vicissitudes. Earlier this year Senator Slade Gorton of Washington State introduced a bill that would work in a similar way.

The fuel for the political firestorm is the perceived threat to private-property rights that results from protecting the habitat of a listed species. In June the Supreme Court gave environmentalists a victory when it upheld federal authority to conserve critical habitats on privately held lands. That protection would be eliminated under the Gorton bill. The research council suggests that the federal government should have a right to make emergency designations of "survival habitat" to protect species in certain cases. But Capitol Hill observers say this idea will probably not go over well in the 104th Congress.

More likely to be successful, perhaps, are approaches advocated by the Keystone Center, a mediating organization that recently published a consensus report on incentives for private landowners to protect species. The center's approach is applauded by Gordon H. Orians of the University of Washington, president of the Ecological Society of America, who observes that environmentalists may have erred in the past by relying too much on command-and-control mechanisms for conservation.

The Keystone Center sees potential for reducing landowners' state tax burden in return for managing their lands in ways that benefit nature. For example, gifts of land containing habitats of an endangered species to conservation organizations could be encouraged by estate tax credits; landowners who entered into voluntary agreements to preserve species could be given income tax credits. Although such approaches reduce government revenues, they may allow protection of endangered species to move forward.

Web Sites

Due to the changing nature of Internet links, the Rosen Publishing Group, Inc., has developed an online list of Web sites related to the subject of this book. This site is updated regularly. Please use this link to access the list:

http://www.rosenlinks.com/saca/enpr

For Further Reading

Ackerman, Diane. *The Rarest of the Rare*. New York, NY: Random House, 1995.

Broecker, Wallace. *How to Build a Habitable Planet.* New York, NY: Columbia University Press, 1998.

Brower, Michael, and Warren Leon. *The Consumer's Guide to Effective Environmental Choices: Practical Advice from the Union of Concerned Scientists.* New York, NY: Three Rivers Press, 1999.

Carson, Rachel. *Silent Spring.* New York, NY: Houghton Mifflin Company, 1962.

Doolittle, Bev. *The Earth Is My Mother.* New York, NY: Greenwich Workshop Press, 2000.

Gleick, Peter. *The World's Water 2004–2005.* Washington, DC: Island Press, 2004.

Graedel, T. E., Paul J. Crutzen, and Thomas E. Graedel. *Atmosphere, Climate, and Change.* New York, NY: W. H. Freeman and Company, 1997.

Locker, Thomas. *Rachel Carson: Preserving a Sense of Wonder.* Golden, CO: Fulcrum Publishing, 2004.

MacKay, Richard. *The Penguin Atlas of Endangered Species: A Worldwide Guide to Plants and Animals.* New York, NY: Penguin Books, 2002.

McDonough, William, and Michael Braungart. *Cradle to Cradle: Remaking the Way We Make Things.* New York, NY: North Point Press, 2002.

Mongillo, John, and Peter Mongillo. *Earth Systems and Ecology* (Teen Guides to Environmental Science). Westport, CT: Greenwood Press, 2004.

Quammen, David. *The Song of the Dodo: Island Biogeography in an Age of Extinctions.* New York, NY: Scribner, 1997.

Schor, Juliet, and Betsy Taylor, eds. *Sustainable Planet: Solutions for the Twenty-first Century.* Boston, MA: Beacon Press, 2003.

Wilson, Edward O. *Biodiversity.* Washington, DC: National Academy Press, 1992.

Wilson, Edward O. *The Future of Life.* New York, NY: Random House, 2002.

Wolverton, B. C. *How to Grow Fresh Air*. New York, NY: Penguin Books, 2004.

Worldwatch Institute. *State of the World 2005: Global Security*. New York, NY: W. W. Norton & Company, Inc., 2005.

Bibliography

Alpert, Mark. "Replumbing the Everglades." *Scientific American*, August 1999, pp. 16–18.

Ashley, Steven. "It's Not Easy Being Green." *Scientific American*, April 2002, pp. 32–34.

Beardsley, Tim. "Endangered Again." *Scientific American*, October 1995, p. 34.

Beyl, Caula A. "Rachel Carson, Silent Spring, and the Environmental Movement." 1991. Retrieved September 28, 2005 (http://www.hort.purdue.edu/newcrop/history/lecture31/r_31-3.html).

Boyd, Claude E. "Notes from an Adviser to the Shrimp Industry." *Scientific American Presents: The Oceans*, Fall 1998, pp. 66–67.

Clay, Jason W. "Comments from an Environmental Advocate." *Scientific American Presents: The Oceans*, Fall 1998, p. 67.

Dinerstein, E., A. Weakley, R. Noss, R. Tipton, and K. Wolfe. World Wildlife Fund. "Everglades." 2001. Retrieved September 28, 2005 (http://www.worldwildlife.org/wildworld/profiles/terrestrial/nt/nt0904_full.html).

The Editors. "The Promise and Perils of Aquaculture." *Scientific American Presents: The Oceans*, Fall 1998, pp. 64–65.

The Editors. "Giant Questions about Shrimp." *Scientific American Presents: The Oceans*, Fall 1998, pp. 66–67.

Environmental Protection Agency. "Six Common Air Pollutants." Retrieved September 28, 2005 (http://www.epa.gov/air/urbanair/nox/).

Gibbs, W. Wayt. "Sewage Treatment Plants." *Scientific American*, November 1995, p. 42.

Graham, Sarah. "Satellites Showed CFC Ban Slowed Ozone Destruction." *Scientific American*, July 30, 2003. Retrieved September 28, 2005 (http://www.sciam.com/article.cfm?articleID = 000D19A5-F60B-1F26-8D4A80A84189EEDF).

Hansen, James. "Defusing the Global Warming Time Bomb." *Scientific American*, March 2004, pp. 68–77.

Herzog, Howard, Baldur Eliasson, and Olav Kaarstad. "Capturing Greenhouse Gases." *Scientific American*, February 2000, pp. 72–79.

Holloway, Marguerite. "Sustaining the Amazon." *Scientific American*, July 1993, pp. 90–99.

Malle, Karl-Geert. "Cleaning Up the River Rhine." *Scientific American*, January 1996, pp. 70–75.

Martindale, Diane. "Car Parts from Chickens." *Scientific American*, April 2000, p. 26.

McKinsey, Krista. "Struggles with Salmon." *Scientific American Presents: The Oceans*, Fall 1998, pp. 68–69.

National Endangered Species Act Reform Coalition. "How NESARC Got Started." Retrieved September 28, 2005 (http://www.nesarc.org/start.htm).

Nemecek, Sasha. "Profile: Mario Molina." *Scientific American*, November 1997, pp. 40–43.

Postel, Sandra. "Growing More Food with Less Water." *Scientific American*, February 2001, pp. 46–51.

Renner, Rebecca. "A Case of the Vapors." *Scientific American*, July 2002, pp. 27–28.

Rice, Richard E., Raymond E. Gullison, and John W. Reid. "Can Sustainable Management Save Tropical Forests?" *Scientific American*, April 1997, pp. 44–49.

Wang, Linda. "Paving Out Pollution." *Scientific American*, February 2002, p. 20.

Whipple, Chris G. "Can Nuclear Waste Be Stored Safely at Yucca Mountain?" *Scientific American*, June 1996, pp. 72–79.

Index

A

ABB, 23, 37
Adams, E. Eric, 28
Adelman, Morris, 12
aerosols, 34, 50, 51, 52, 55,
    58, 59, 60, 61–62
AES, 15
air pollution, 7, 39–40,
    40–42, 59, 61, 74, 75, 159
Amazon rain forest, conserv-
    ing, 163–164, 164–186
Anderson, Anthony B., 169,
    170, 173–174, 180
Appelbaum, Stuart, 208
aquaculture/fish farms, 8,
    91, 92–95
  salmon farming, 91, 95,
    102–107
  shrimp farming, 91, 95,
    96–97, 97–99, 100–102
Army Corps of Engineers,
    204, 205–208
Asahi, Ryoji, 42
Association of Southeast
    Asian Nations Fisheries
    Network, 99
Australian Prawn Farmers
    Association, 99

B

Babbitt, Bruce, 206
Barreto, Paulo, 175, 180
biological oxygen
    demand, 118

C

carbon dioxide, 11–12, 13, 14,
    42, 43, 46, 47, 48, 49, 55,
    59, 60, 61, 64–65, 121
  storing/sequestering,
    14–38, 65
carbon sequestering,
    14–38, 65
CARE, 15
Cargill-Dow Polymers, 129
Carson, Rachel, 5–6, 9, 10
chemical oxygen demand, 118
chlorinated solvents, 159,
    160–162
chlorine compounds, 118–120
chlorofluorocarbons, 11, 43,
    59, 67–68, 68–75
Clark, David B., 185
Clean Air Act, 71
Clinton, Bill, 74
Conservation Inter-
    national, 168

About the Editor

Krista West earned an M.A. degree in earth science at Lamont-Doherty Earth Observatory, Columbia University, New York; an M.S. degree in journalism from Columbia University's Graduate School of Journalism; and a B.S. degree in zoology from the University of Washington in Seattle. She writes on topics about the earth sciences and environment for various science magazines, including *Scientific American* and *Natural History Magazine*. Ms. West lives and works in Fairbanks, Alaska.

Illustration Credits

Cover © Gabe Palmer/Corbis; pp. 17, 18–19, 26, 32 David Fierstein; p. 47 Jen Christiansen (Source: J. R. Petit et al. in *Nature*, vol. 399, pp. 429–436; June 3, 1999); pp. 53, 55, 64 Jen Christiansen (Source: James Hansen); p. 73 Bryan Christie; pp. 96, 142–143 Roberto Osti; p. 119 Dimitry Schidlovsky; p. 167 Johnny Johnson.

Series Designer: Tahara Anderson
Series Editor: Kathy Kuhtz Campbell